Praise for
The Sending Church

A church that lives within its four walls isn't a church at all. *The Sending Church* by Pat Hood will challenge pastors and church leaders not to just grow the church but to equip its members to live on mission.

Mark Batterson, *New York Times*
best-selling author of *The Circle Maker*

Pat Hood provides a convicting look into what happens when God's kingdom—not our own kingdom—becomes our passion. This book will be instrumental in shaping leaders, churches, and denominations toward a heart for the kingdom.

Kevin Ezell, President
North American Mission Board

A story about a church's success would never capture my attention, but a story about God awakening His bride to His mission is mesmerizing. Don't read this book intending to discover a formula for your church's success, but as a challenge to listen and yield to God's mission.

Jeff Lewis, Assistant Professor of
Intercultural Studies, California Baptist University

Under Pat's leadership, God has transformed LifePoint into a church that sends to the nations, both locally and globally. We and innumerable others have learned so much from them about what it means to be a Sending Church. Their story, represented in these pages, is remarkable. It is truly a must-read.

Larry McCrary, cofounder
Upstream Collective

The Sending Church is a story of church revitalization and Great Commission transformation. I recommend this book to any pastor or church member who wants to see their church catch fire with passion for reaching the nations for Christ.

Ed Stetzer, author of *Subversive Kingdom* and President of LifeWay Research

the
Sending
church

THE CHURCH MUST
LEAVE THE BUILDING

the **Sending** church

PAT HOOD

PUBLISHING GROUP

NASHVILLE, TENNESSEE

Published by B&H Publishing Group

Nashville, Tennessee

Dewey Decimal Classification: 269.2

Subject Heading: MISSIONS / EVANGELISTIC
WORK \ CHURCH

1 2 3 4 5 6 7 8 • 17 16 15 14 13

Contents

Acknowledgments

WHEN I THINK ABOUT all the people who played an important role in making this book a reality, I'm humbled and honored to have so many to thank.

Amy, you are an amazing wife. Thank you for the countless sacrifices you've made throughout the years of the ministry God has called us to. Thank you for being a rock star among pastors' wives. Thank you for loving me unconditionally and supporting me in the good times and . . . the not-so-good times. Thank you for always being by my side and for having my back. Thank you for loving Jesus so much, because I know you could never love me like you do if you didn't love Him like you do.

Kyle Goen, you are an amazing friend. Thank you for faithfully serving with me for so many years. Thank you for your commitment to go to war for the glory of God. Thank you for your important role in helping shape the vision for *The Sending Church*.

My staff, thank you, men and women, for your loyalty and commitment to serve our Savior by my side. Thank you for running hard after the heart of God and His heart for the nations.

Dino Senesi, I cannot express my gratitude for how you stepped in at the eleventh hour to make this book a reality. You have become an amazing friend through this project. Thank you for your patience and your persistence.

Leslie Overby, thank you for serving as my assistant for so many years. Your role in my ministry cannot be measured. Thank you for being not just an assistant, but a ministry partner called to serve alongside me. I'm forever indebted and grateful to you.

Ken Hubbard, tears form in my eyes just thinking of this great man. I'm blessed that God ordained this man to be a part of my life. I'm a better pastor and leader because of his influence. There is no way this book would become a reality without his bold leadership and investment in a young minister.

Finally, the LifePoint community. Thank you for your commitment to the global glory of God. Thank you for leaving the building. Thank you for not playing church games. Thank you for being global Christians, not consumer Christians. Thank you for being more passionate about the glory of God than the preferences of man.

Introduction

ELVIS DIED WHEN I was eleven years old. He was known as the king of rock and roll. Funny thing is, I still remember the reaction of our nation. It was truly befitting of a king. Everyone was in shock. The world, at least the world I knew, seemed to stop for a moment to catch its breath.

Even with all of today's technology, rock stars still can't top the energy or excitement of a live Elvis Presley show. Even after his show ended, people refused to leave. They would remain in the auditorium and scream his name, hoping for an encore. After several minutes, in order to get fans to leave the building, the announcer would proclaim, "Elvis has left the building."

That's what *The Sending Church* is all about. No, it's not about Elvis leaving the building; it's a plea for the church to leave the building. Sadly, like starstruck Elvis fans, the local church doesn't seem to want to leave the building. I'm not talking about going home to eat lunch after the gathering on Sunday; I'm talking about leaving the building to join Jesus in the incredible mission of disciple making.

In his book *The Knowledge of the Holy*, A. W. Tozer said, "What comes to mind when we think about God is the most important thing about us." What we believe about God will determine how we work at our jobs, how we treat our families, and how we spend our money. What we believe about God will determine everything about our lives.

I believe the same is true for the church. What we believe about church is crazy important because it will determine how we spend our money, what we promote, what we preach, and what we challenge our people to do.

In the Old Testament, God's Spirit hadn't yet been poured out (Joel 2:28) on His people because Jesus had not yet atoned for the sins of those who surrender to Him. So, God's presence dwelled among His people in a place called the Holy of Holies, in the innermost part of the tabernacle. All the religious activity revolved around the tabernacle or temple. If people wanted to meet with God, they went to the temple. If people wanted to offer sacrifices for their sins, they went to the temple. Every aspect of the people's relationship with God revolved around going to a place.

In the Gospels, the presence of God dwelled in a person—Jesus. Then, from the book of Acts onward, after the death and resurrection of Jesus, the Holy Spirit invades the lives of all whose heart's He captures (Acts 2). The presence of God now indwells all believers.

This reality should radically change our concept of church. Church is no longer a building we go to; it's a community of people redeemed by the sacrifice of Jesus and commissioned to the task of going out of the building to take the gospel to the nations.

In order to obey the commands of Jesus, the church must leave the building.

The church in Acts "got it." They gathered to magnify the goodness of the exalted King, but they understood their task was to leave the building. At first, they didn't go across the ocean; they were focused on going across the street. Their lives were so radically transformed by the gospel that they didn't see their faith as connected to a place; it was life. As a result, the church grew exponentially.

This book is an attempt to challenge the church to leave the building. We must move beyond Sunday. If we hope to make a difference in a hopeless world, our people must go and the church must send.

This is the story of how God transformed my church into a Sending Church and followed the King out of the building.

Chapter 1

Unstoppable

*And thus I make it my ambition to preach
the gospel, not where Christ has already
been named, lest I build on someone else's
foundation, but as it is written, "Those who
have never been told of him will see, and those
who have never heard will understand."*

(ROMANS 15:20–21)

LIKE MANY OTHER FOURTEEN-YEAR-OLD boys, Whit
didn't come to LifePoint to study the Bible and find
Jesus; he came to ride his skateboard and find a girl.
Every Wednesday night, hundreds of teenagers flock to
LifePoint like hippies to Woodstock. Some come because

they love Jesus, and others because they love to have a good time. Whit didn't come because he loved Jesus. But that soon changed.

Whit was surprised when he found himself asking questions about the Bible and drawn into the stories of Jesus. He got involved in a small group with a leader that began to pour into his life. Through this relationship, Whit realized that life was about more than adrenaline and cute blondes. God invaded Whit's heart and drastically transformed his life. Rather than chasing after the heart of a girl, he began to chase after the heart of God.

By the time Whit was in college, he knew that God had created him for something bigger than the American dream. At a time when most students are trying to position themselves to get all they can out of life, Whit was positioning himself to give his life away.

LifePoint developed a partnership with a ministry called Community Servants (www.communityservants.org) at a local housing community full of first-generation refugees. We received several rent-free apartments. In exchange, we helped college interns move in. These interns would have a continual ministry presence in the community by developing after-school programs, ESL classes, and other mercy ministries for the residents.

Whit was one of the first students to move in, roll up his sleeves, and get busy. God used this experience to capture his heart for His glory among the nations. So, when many college students are spending their daddy's money to lie on a beach during summer break, Whit raised money so he could serve the poorest of the poor in the "favelas" of Sao Paulo, Brazil.

"God has shown me why I have a mouth to speak, a heart that pumps blood, and lungs to breathe air," Whit recently said. "I exist for the sole purpose of being used as a tool for God's glory. I was not saved to be silent."

Whit found that, just as Jesus taught, giving your life away is the only way to find real life. After returning from a summer serving in the slums of Brazil, Whit moved to Brussels, Belgium, to serve as a year-long intern at LifePoint Brussels. He is so passionate about making God famous that he is willing to take online classes so he can help plant churches in a place where the gospel is as scarce as water in a dry desert.

Whit is definitely living a sent life. I don't know where Whit will end up next; neither does he. But, I know what he will be doing when he gets there—giving his life away to make God famous.

When Do I Leave?

Bret never left the United States until he was forty-four years old; he didn't even have a passport. The first time he left the country was when he traveled to San Paulo, Brazil, to serve in the same slums that Whit served during his summer break.

Like most people, Bret went to Brazil thinking he would get the opportunity to help hurting people. Also, like most people, Bret came home with a different perspective. He did amazing things for a lot of people in great need. But, these people did much more for Bret than he could ever do for them. Like Whit, God used this experience to explode Bret's heart for God's glory among the nations. Over the next four years, he sacrificed his vacation to personally lead twelve mission trips to Brazil. Bret didn't want to just take up space; he wanted to get busy.

Although you would never know it because of his humble lifestyle, Bret was making a six-figure income with five-figure yearly bonuses working for a commercial construction company. He was such a valued employee that his company wanted to promote him to vice president. Most men wouldn't have to think or even "pray" about it. (Talk about a no-brainer!) But, then again, Bret doesn't think like most men.

Bret doesn't live for position or possessions; Bret lives for something greater, something bigger. He didn't exactly know why at the moment, but Brett said, "Thanks, but no thanks, it's not what I want to do with my life."

His boss was shocked. Only a fool would turn down that kind of promotion and money. He was right—Bret is a fool . . . a fool for Christ. Bret didn't know exactly what it was, but he knew God was leading him to something greater.

On his next mission trip to Brazil, Bret became restless and frustrated. He was tithing and giving a lot of money to missions. He was serving locally and globally. He was teaching and serving on LifePoint's Board of Directors. His whole life revolved around the things of God. So, why was he still so restless?

In his frustration, Bret went out on a mountain beside our mission house in Brazil and cried out to God, "Lord, I give money. I go. I teach. What do You what me to do? Do You want me to give more?"

What a question! This is every pastor's dream—a guy making a lot of money asking God if he should be giving more. Do cops love donuts? YES! Seriously, don't blow by that question. The question most people ask is, "God, when do I get more?" Bret asked, "Lord, do You want me to give more?" The questions we ask often reveal the condition of our heart. On that hill, surrounded by the brokenness of the world, Bret sensed God say, "I don't want your money. I want your life."

Bret came home, sold his house, quit his job, and moved to Brazil. His life was no longer about building buildings for a paycheck; his life was about building relationships for God's glory. He left behind success, friends, home, and aging parents to live a sent life for the global glory of God.

"Yes" on the Table

After a year in Brazil, Bret and Susie returned to the States for a visit. As Bret and I debriefed their work in Brazil, Bret shared that he felt God leading them to go to a place where the gospel was not known.

I asked Bret if he was open to anywhere. He didn't hesitate. He said "YES," as if to say, "Why do you even have to ask?" So, I shared our vision of sending a team to Bangkok, Thailand, to reach the millions of unreached people in that city and region for the gospel and asked Bret if he would pray about being the team leader for LifePoint Bangkok.

I'll never forget Bret's response. He said, "God has directed me to go to unreached people. Your question is the answer to my prayer of where. When do I leave?" Bret had laid his YES on the table before he even asked the question.

Living for the Pleasure of God

Ashley is another example of living a sent life. She came to LifePoint as a college student and quickly connected to a small group. She saw other college students serving as interns at the same housing project where Whit was serving. Like Whit, she was captivated by others who were living a sent life.

She wanted to get involved, but she was afraid of what she would have to give up. So, she decided to wade in the shallow end by spending an occasional afternoon serving in the community. As with Whit, Ashley was hooked. She found herself giving more and more time and life away. She finally jumped in the deep end and moved in to serve daily as an intern.

After graduating from college, most young men and women are ready to tackle life and start making money. But God had transformed Ashley's ambitions. Her friends were getting jobs and moving into nice apartments. But Ashley couldn't bear the thought of moving out of a community that she had given so much of her life to—and that had given her so much more back in return.

So, rather than getting a job and moving into a "nicer" neighborhood, Ashley followed a countercultural career path. She took a job as a ministry assistant in our student ministry and rented an apartment in the housing project so she could continue to live a sent life.

Ashley now spends her time teaching adult ESL classes to international refugees in order to help them have the needed skills to survive their new world . . . but that's not really why she does it. She simply uses ESL as a platform to build relationships through which she can share the gospel.

Ashley chose to give her life away by serving those who have grown up in a world very different from her own—a world filled with war, hate, and persecution. She serves those who once feared daily for their lives in their home country and have lost countless loved ones.

Recently, she told me about a conversation with a twelve-year-old boy in the community. He told her that if he were still living in his home country, he would be forced to be a soldier and carry a gun. She was profoundly moved.

Here is a glimpse into Ashley's heart:

> When people ask me why in the world I would choose to live in such a place, I just look at them and smile. What they don't realize is that I can't

imagine living anywhere else. Being a missionary doesn't always mean dropping everything and moving halfway across the world. Sometimes it just means being intentional in building relationships with the people you encounter every day. It's not about being perfect, but it is about following God. It is about serving others even when you're tired and don't feel like it. It's about putting others first and giving up your own desires so that you can love on people.

Many nights, Ashley comes home exhausted from a long day at the office. The last thing she wants to do is spend two hours teaching English. Like every other single girl her age, I'm sure she'd like to go out with friends or just relax at home. But, rather than her own pleasure, she's committed to living for the pleasure of God.

Whit, a college kid living his "glory years" when most kids try to get all they can out of life, is giving his life away by living for the glory of God among the nations. Bret didn't kick off the second half of life by buying a red convertible or trading his wife in on a newer model. He turned down a promotion, sold everything he had, left behind his aging parents, and moved to another culture to make disciples and plant churches for the glory of God among the nations. Ashley gave up the American dream in exchange for experiencing the riches of God's pleasure. All three have one thing in common: they make up the unstoppable church.

The Unstoppable Church

Most people today, both inside and outside the church, have no clue why the church exists. But, by reading these stories of the incredible life-change experienced by Whit, Bret, and Ashley, I hope you get a clue.

Their value system has been completely revolutionized. Their distaste for things that most people in our culture love feels, at times . . . un-American. Ambitions no longer make sense. Goals shift. Passions evolve. Why? All for Jesus, His mission, and His glory.

When I describe the church as "unstoppable," the conversation changes. What does *unstoppable* mean?

Unstoppable: not capable of being stopped; extremely forceful[1]

Jesus didn't establish the church to be weak and defeated. Excuses for our lack of effectiveness must die. He designed and empowered the church to be unstoppable. What I love about the definition is that there is no mention of defense; it's all offense . . . "extremely forceful."

We are not an anxious band of wounded warriors trying to hold our ground against an evil enemy. We are created to advance the mission of God. The churches that really get this cause the demons in hell to literally shake in their boots.

As people's lives are radically changed by the grace and mercy of Jesus, the advance goes viral. I love the implications of what Jesus told His disciples before He left them, as recorded by Luke in the book of Acts:

> But you will receive power when the Holy Spirit has come upon you, and you will be my witnesses in Jerusalem and in all Judea and Samaria, and to the end of the earth. (Acts 1:8)

Notice, Jesus predicted three things would happen as the unstoppable church was birthed. Jesus' disciples would:

1. Receive power
2. Become His witnesses
3. Advance the gospel to the end of the earth

In Matthew 28:19–20, we read the commission of God described by Jesus:

> Go therefore and make disciples of all nations, baptizing them in the name of the Father and of

the Son and of the Holy Spirit, teaching them to observe all I have commanded you. And behold, I am with you always, to the end of the age.

Acts 1:8 and Matthew 28:19–20 aren't just for spiritual superstars; they give a picture of what should be normative for every believer and every church.

Every believer has been indwelled by the Holy Spirit and empowered to go be His witnesses in every domain of life. As believers obey these commands, the church will be impossible to contain to a building, city, country, or a continent. The church will be an unstoppable force.

Current Realities

The American church does not seem unstoppable today. When we look at the effect of the culture on the church, it's obvious that we have become marginalized. We seem to be missing the vision of Jesus as to what the empowered, unstoppable church should look like. As a result, it's sexy for people to claim to love Jesus, but not His church.

I hear it all the time, especially among younger generations. They describe the church as: hypocritical and judgmental, just wanting people's money, more focused on bigger buildings than on the needs of hurting people, more interested in the condition of people's clothes than the condition of their hearts, and too narrow-minded. The list could go on for pages and pages.

I understand that the institutional church is what critics are normally describing, not necessarily the church that Jesus established. I also understand that we who lead churches are partly responsible for creating these bad vibes, and that makes me sick. By our action and inaction, we have vastly underachieved as His church.

Because the church is made up of individual believers, the problems most critics bark about are personal obedience problems. Would critics have wind in their sails if those who claim to love Jesus actually lived like it? Would people think the church is irrelevant if church members worried more about people's hearts than their appearance?

Would the critic cry foul if the church actually went to the world rather than expecting the world to come to us? How would the reputation of Jesus' bride change if the church worked harder proclaiming what we are *for* than what we are against? What would happen if, rather than fighting for personal desires and preferences, church members fought for the glory and fame of God?

As a result of their disenchantment with the institutional church, many of the "love Jesus/hate the church" crowd have even tried to redefine what the church means.

Some define church as simply plural for "Christian." If a few believers get together over a cup of coffee, that's church. But, I believe if church is anything you want it to be, then church is nothing—or just a creation of Christians searching for a support group.

Many new church planting movements are birthed out of discontentment with the current realities of modern church culture. The new movements are not necessarily bad, but we can't let them become a Trojan horse filled with consumer Christians. It takes a lot less money to buy a homeless man a bicycle than to send a missionary family to Thailand to live among the poor. Designer Christianity based on the opinions of a small group at Starbucks is no different that the "Six Flags over Jesus" megachurch. Both can fall victim to "Have It Your Way" Christianity.

Multiple forms of church can support and multiply biblical Christians—I believe that. But biblical Christianity includes self-denial. Biblical Christianity also includes ethnic, economic, and social diversity, not just a group of cookie cutters sitting in a coffee shop (or church building). The early church lived in community and shared everything they had. Read the book of Acts. There was nothing easy or comfortable about the church being the church in a Christless culture.

Unstoppable DNA

Although the church is encoded by Jesus to be unstoppable, we are losing influence in the world. Estimates say only 17 percent of Americans attend a "Christian" church on a given Sunday, and the number will drop to 14 percent by 2020. The term *Christian* in the research is given a much broader designation than most of us would agree with. In that same seven-year period an estimated 55,000 churches will close.[2]

Less than 20 percent of churches are growing and only 1 percent are growing by reaching lost people. The other 99 percent are growing by gaining people from other churches.[3] That doesn't sound very unstoppable to me.

Legendary football coach Vince Lombardi once started training camp by holding up a football and saying, "Gentlemen, this is a football." To discover the "unstoppable" strain in the church's DNA, we have to return to the basics. I'm going old-school Lombardi on you:

Ladies and gentlemen, this is a church.

The first time the word *church* is used in the Bible is by Jesus in Matthew:

Simon Peter replied, "You are the Christ, the Son of the living God." And Jesus answered him,

"Blessed are you, Simon Bar-jonah! For flesh and blood has not revealed this to you, but my Father who is in heaven. And I tell you, you are Peter, and on this rock I will build my *church*, and the gates of hell shall not prevail against it." (Matt. 16:16–18, emphasis added)

This passage clearly describes the church and the offensive juggernaut that Jesus has empowered us to be.

Unstoppable Jesus

Peter's confession, "You are the Christ, the Son of the living God," put Jesus as the unstoppable force driving the local church. Paul explained:

He is the image of the invisible God, the first-born of all creation. For by him all things were created, in heaven and on earth, visible and invisible, whether thrones or dominions or rulers or authorities—all things were created through him and for him. And he is before all things, and in him all things hold together. And he is the head of the body, the church. He is the beginning, the firstborn from the dead, that in everything he might be preeminent. For in him all the fullness of God was pleased to dwell, and through him to reconcile to himself all things, whether on earth or in heaven, making peace by the blood of his cross. (Col. 1:15–20)

A biblical understanding of both Jesus and the church is mission critical because the biblical church is all about Jesus. And, because Jesus is unstoppable, so is His church.

You Can't Love Jesus without Loving the Church

Do you remember when Saul was trying to stop the church by persecuting Jesus' disciples? He was on his way to Damascus to persecute Christians when Jesus struck him blind and asked, "Saul, why are you persecuting Me?" Sounds strange at first read because the Bible doesn't say Saul was persecuting Jesus:

"And there arose on that day a great persecution against the *church* in Jerusalem." (Acts 8:1, emphasis added)

"But Saul, still breathing threats and murder against the *disciples of the Lord.*" (Acts 9:1, emphasis added)

Jesus asked Saul why "He" was being persecuted because the church belongs to Jesus. Remember, in Matthew 16, Jesus said, "I will build my church." LifePoint doesn't belong to its pastor or the people who attend. It belongs to Jesus. So, if you mess with the church, you mess with Jesus. Think about that the next time you decide to "hate on the church but love Jesus."

Love them both or hate them both, but you can't love one without loving the other because the church belongs to Jesus. He established the church, loves the church, and purchased the church with His own blood.

Immediately after Jesus celebrated Peter's answer, He told the disciples He must go to Jerusalem and die. Peter said, "Not on my watch." Jesus rebuked him and said, "Get behind me, Satan! You are a hindrance to me" (Matt. 16:23).

Doesn't that sound crazy? Peter was praised by Jesus one moment and scolded the next. Satan is a master of disguise. He will do anything to stop the church, or at least distract the church from her mission.

As Peter learned, we're either on God's mission or the enemy's mission. When we do what we want instead of what Jesus wants, we're on the enemy's mission. When people are more concerned with their personal prefer- ences and interests than the heart of God, they have switched sides. If someone attacks the doctrine or direction of the church that is in alignment with the will of God as revealed in Scripture, they're on the enemy's mission.

The lordship of Christ is the first pillar of the church.

Jesus said, "I will build My church." How does Jesus build His church? He builds His church by making disciples. The word *petros* is translated "Peter" and means "pebble." The word for rock was *petra*, which means a rock bed.

So, basically, Jesus was saying, "I'll build My church on those who surrender to Me." Peter later affirmed, "You yourselves like living stones are being built up as a spiritual house" (1 Pet. 2:5).

There are some who think Peter became the first pope at this moment. Yeah, and every boy becomes a man when he turns eighteen.

Jesus is the cornerstone of the church, not Peter. Jesus taught that the first pillar of the church is people who profess Jesus as "the Christ, the Son of the living God." The church isn't a group of people who gather to listen to good music and hear a good motivational speech. The church isn't necessarily those who have been baptized and signed on the dotted line of membership. As a matter of fact, I've heard estimates that 50 percent of church members aren't true believers, and I think that's being generous.

The church is the assembly of people redeemed by Jesus because they believe He is God in flesh and lived a perfect life to die as their substitute. The church consists of people who surrender to Jesus as Lord. So, the church isn't for spectators. It's for people who have "died to self." In other words, they've died to their own agenda, passions, ambitions, and dreams in order to live for the glory and fame of God.

After Peter confessed Jesus as Lord, Jesus blessed him and said, "Flesh and blood has not revealed this to you, but my Father who is in heaven" (Matt. 16:17). In other words, "Don't think you answered correctly because you have a higher IQ than the other disciples. The only reason you got it right is because God opened your eyes to the truth."

Paul later said, "No one can say 'Jesus is Lord' except in the Holy Spirit" (1 Cor. 12:3). We cannot enlighten ourselves any more than we can transform ourselves. So, the first pillar of the church is those who have been redeemed by Jesus, live transformed lives.

Reciting the sinner's prayer doesn't make someone a Christian any more than reciting the Pledge of Allegiance makes someone an American. No magical incantation is powerful enough to change our eternal destiny. Salvation is about total surrender to the lordship of Jesus that transforms you into the image of Jesus.

The authority of Scripture is the second pillar of the church.

Many people think spiritually maturity is determined by how much Bible you know. But, knowing the Bible doesn't equate spiritual maturity. The enemy knows more of God's Word than any preacher or seminary professor on the planet, and he's going to spend eternity begging for ice water.

Spiritual maturity is not determined by how much Bible you *know*; spiritual maturity is determined by how much Bible you *do*. That's why James said, "But be doers of the word, and not hearers only, deceiving yourselves" (James 1:22).

Spiritual maturity is determined by transformation not information. How much do you love what God loves, and hate what He hates? How much of God's Word are you willing to obey, no matter the cost? Those questions will help you determine if God is at work, transforming you into His image.

Show me a church committed to these two things—lordship and biblical obedience—and I will show you a church that is making an impact in their community and around the world. I will show you a church that is living out the vision of Jesus as seen in Acts 1:8.

Offense, Not Defense

Jesus said the "gates of hell will not prevail" against the church. The phrase "gates of hell" is a euphemism for death. Death will not prevail against the church. In other words, contrary to the naysayers and church critics, the church will never die. Beware of people who are not afraid to die. They are unstoppable!

Many people read this phrase and think the church is on defense against the attacks of hell. But, the church isn't on defense; it's on offense. Notice, Jesus said, "The gates of hell will not prevail."

Think about that phrase. Gates aren't offensive—they're defensive. They keep people out. In other words, Jesus is saying hell cannot stop the church from advancing. Jesus' church will ultimately accomplish what He established us to do . . . make disciples of all nations.

Jesus' disciples learned that they were created to play offense, not defense. After Jesus was crucified and buried in a borrowed tomb, His disciples went into hiding. They were on defense, holed up until the heat died down

(John 20:19–20). Sadly, this is a familiar picture of many churches today.

But, after Jesus defeated death and spent forty days teaching His disciples, He told them, "I'm going back to heaven to be with the Father, but you stay in Jerusalem until you receive the Holy Spirit."

Acts 2 tells the story of the Holy Spirit invading the lives of those who surrendered to Jesus. Suddenly, the church had peace, purpose, and the Holy Spirit. That's all it needed to quit playing defense and start playing offense. As a result, history will never be the same. Although they were jailed, boiled, beheaded, and crucified upside down, they were unstoppable.

We talk about Jesus today because those fearful disciples were transformed into fearless soldiers, empowered to keep on marching. Even death did not slow them down. That's why we must be a Sending Church. We must send people into homes, neighborhoods, workplaces, schools, social circles, and to the ends of the earth because people are counting on us to be unstoppable for Jesus!

Far from Perfect

As I think of the incredible God stories, like the three in this chapter, I feel blessed. I'm living every pastor's dream; I'm watching men and women of all ages give their lives away. I'm blessed to lead a group of people that don't want to just "play" church or "go" to church; they want to "be" the church.

We still have our share of knuckleheads. We have Christian consumers who are more interested in what we can do for them than what they can do for the church. We have husbands who lose their minds, leave their wives, and run out on their kids. We have people who want to sing "Onward Christian Soldiers" every Sunday but run away from the battles in their own lives during the week. We have people who love to sing "Amazing Grace" but never give grace to their neighbors.

My point is, we're far from perfect. Like any church, we're made up of people who were born totally depraved as a result of the Fall. But, we're blessed to have a large group of people who don't see the church as a building we attend—but as a people who are sent.

This wasn't always the case, and getting here hasn't been easy. But seeing people run hard after the heart of God as part of His unstoppable church makes it more than worth it.

✝ *LifePoints . . .*

I first felt led to missions when I was a senior in high school. Since that time I have done four out-of-the-country mission internships through LifePoint in Brazil, Haiti, West Africa, and Thailand. LifePoint has so many opportunities to serve those locally and globally. I now understand what it means to be a disciple of Christ and what it means to disciple others. **—Erica**

～～～～～

LifePoint has cast that vision that "Life Is Missions." It's not just a summer abroad in Brazil or a one-week trip to China. It's life. It's every day. Missions happens at work, school, and the grocery store. When loving God and loving others is the priority in your life, then your life embodies missions. **—Brittany**

～～～～～

God has truly used LifePoint to get me off the sidelines. A lifelong church attender/member, I was mainly satisfied with my "I'm here, feed me" lifestyle as a believer. LifePoint consistently reflects a bias toward action, a willingness to change, and a commitment toward making God famous in the world. **—Tim**

Moving Forward . . .

1. What is your biggest fear about putting your "yes" on the table for Jesus?

2. How could you address that fear more effectively?

Chapter 2

Courageous

This Book of the Law shall not depart from your mouth, but you shall meditate on it day and night, so that you may be careful to do according to all that is written in it. For then you will make your way prosperous, and then you will have good success.

(JOSHUA 1:8)

THANKSGIVING 1993 WAS NOT a normal Thanksgiving for the Hood family. I loaded up my two sons (Seth and Zac) and my wife (Amy) and drove 600 miles from Greenville, Texas, to Smyrna, Tennessee, to interview with the committee charged with finding the next youth pastor at First Baptist Church (FBC), Smyrna.

I was about to cross the finish line in a grueling marathon called seminary. I was young and had a few years' experience, the combination every church desires in a youth minister. So, I felt like a five-star high school football recruit with pastors calling almost every night trying to convince me to be their next youth pastor. One of those pastors was Ken Hubbard, Pastor of FBC, Smyrna. He'd gotten my name from my best friend, Kyle Goen, who was a youth minister in Florida.

Kyle and I met while standing in line to register on the first day of our first semester at seminary. We instantly bonded. We were like Maverick and Goose in Top Gun; I was always reckless and wide-open while Kyle was cautious and calculating. It didn't take long to realize that we made a pretty good team. We spent the next couple of years laughing, dreaming, and skipping chapel to hang out at our favorite Fort Worth "hole in the wall" all–you-can-eat pancakes joint.

Kyle's home church, First Baptist Church (Greenville, Texas), was looking for a youth pastor and he recommended me for the job. So, I spent the next couple of years preaching a lot of sermons and writing a lot of papers. He graduated a semester before me and snagged a sweet gig as youth pastor of First Baptist Church in Dade City,

Florida. That's where he met Ken Hubbard who was in Dade City to preach a revival at FBC.

Ken needed a youth pastor and it didn't take long for Kyle's strong leadership ability to catch his eye. But, he didn't want to steal Kyle from his buddy, so he asked him for a recommendation. Just like he'd done two years earlier, Kyle recommended me.

Know When to Put on Your Running Shoes

After a lot of prayer, Amy and I felt God leading us to Smyrna, Tennessee. There were absolutely no benefits and the pay wasn't enough for Amy to stay home and take care of our kids, but we knew this is where God wanted us to be.

Before we traveled back to Smyrna, I received a call from a staff member we met on our first visit. He had accepted a position at another church and advised me to steer clear of FBC, Smyrna. He said the church was about to hit some major turbulence because it was stuck in tradition and would never make the changes needed to reach the community. I appreciated his honesty, but I was young and naive and ready for a challenge.

When I told Amy about my phone conversation, she said, "If that's where God is leading, that's where we're going, no matter what." I'm so glad God blessed me and blinded Amy. She's a rock star among pastors' wives.

We kicked off our ministry in Smyrna in February of 1994 and the honeymoon didn't last long. It took all of about two months for me to realize that when a staff member calls and says run in the opposite direction, you might want to put on your running shoes.

I was so discouraged that I actually apologized to Amy for bringing her to Smyrna. I told her if we could hang on for one year, we'd be on the next train out of the station. I felt like we at least owed them that much.

That summer, we loaded up approximately thirty-five students and six adults and drove to South Carolina for our first youth camp. During this trip, God began to change our students into a powerful force that would be the catalyst He would use to change an entire church.

When I arrived, our Wednesday night youth program consisted of fun and games with the obligatory, but brief, Bible study at the end. Obviously, it was time for some major changes. So, we gave Wednesday night an extreme makeover.

Rather than fun and games, we started a rock band with loud music that made many people think I had lost my mind. Some thought I was ruining their kids. I guess you could say they were ruined—ruined for the gospel. By the end of August, our Wednesday night attendance had grown from about 45 to over 150.

But, it wasn't just students that were attracted to our Wednesday night youth service. Many adults began to sneak in and sit in the back. They were drawn to the excitement and secretly loved the energy. Some wondered why we didn't do this on Sunday morning.

Everything was going great. The students were excited. The deacons were excited. Ken was excited. Everybody was excited—until one Wednesday night when I didn't cancel our youth service to take our students to the monthly business meeting.

If you grew up in a Baptist church, then I'm sure you have flashbacks of the monthly business meetings. If you still go to a church with a monthly business meeting, send me a direct message and tell me the war stories. We'll laugh instead of cry and then I'll pray for you.

Our student ministry was blowing, going, and gaining a lot of momentum. We were hitting our target of reaching a lot of unchurched teenagers who knew nothing about Jesus or the church. So, taking them to a business meeting would go one of two ways; they'd either run far away and never come back, or they'd come back at least once a month just to see the fight (sometimes our business meeting rivaled a pay-per-view UFC match). Either way, they'd have a bad perception of what the church is all about.

So, when the monthly business meeting rolled around, I ignored it. To keep it "G" rated, some church culture people weren't too happy with me. Can you imagine the audacity, leading kids to worship rather than taking them to a cage fight? So, I met with our leadership and told them that God had called me to lead students to run hard after the heart of God, not educate them on the fine art of throwing a sucker punch in the name of Christ. Besides, we couldn't gain any momentum or consistency if we cancelled everything once a month.

Finally, they voted to move our monthly business meetings from 7 to 8 p.m. If that seems like a small thing to you, then you've obviously never led a church like ours at the time. People who didn't tithe, share their faith, and barely even knew how to spell J-E-S-U-S were able to have a voice in the decisions and set the direction of the church.

Change Is Good but Never Easy

The staff member who called to warn me of impending doom had left by the time I arrived. A few months later, the Worship Pastor left, leaving Ken and me as the only full-time permanent staff members. The outlook was discouraging, until I met Eddie Mosley.

I was introduced to a young Minister of Education and Youth at a meeting at LifeWay (the Baptist Sunday School Board at the time). I knew immediately that I liked this guy. So, in the middle of a meeting, I wrote a simple question and slid it across the table:

Do you want to play church the rest of your life or do you want a chance to change the world?

Eddie just smiled, but in about a month, he became our Minister of Education.

Not long after Eddie moved to Smyrna, we hired an interim worship pastor named Ron Alley. Ron had a gracious personality and was loved by everyone. So, it didn't take long for Ron to agree to lose the interim title and become our full-time worship pastor.

Like every other church at the time, we had Sunday morning and Sunday evening worship services. I'm sure Sunday evening worship was a good idea at some point in history. But in the church world—more times than not—what starts out as simply *a good idea* transforms into *a biblical command* in the imagination of the congregation, if held on to long enough.

At the time, we averaged about six hundred in our morning worship gatherings and about seventy-five in our Sunday evening gatherings. Our Sunday evening gatherings were sort of like warmed leftovers—they taste similar to what you had earlier, but you don't expect it to be quite as good.

Our young staff knew we needed to become more relevant to our young and rapidly growing community. So, Ron started wading into the shallow end of the "change pool" by adding a guitar and drums to our piano and organ on Sunday night. Then, he started singing songs that weren't even in the hymnbook. Some said he had a demon, others said he was a heretic. But, a strange thing happened.

Our Sunday evening service grew from about seventy-five "frozen chosen" who would rather be somewhere else, to two hundred energetic people who sang with a smile on their face and conviction in their voice. Sunday night became the talk of the church and the community. One of our older deacons named Jim told me:

> Son, people all over town are talking about what's happening here. This place is rockin' like a honky-tonk on Friday night and that ain't a bad thing.

Everyone didn't share Jim's enthusiasm, especially when we waded out a little deeper and put a projector and screen in the auditorium. The frozen chosen started complaining and threatened to take their tithe to another church if we didn't stop this madness.

The warning call I received before coming to Smyrna kept ringing in my ears. Even though things were going great in our student ministry and we were growing in all areas of the church, I still secretly wished to be somewhere else. I needed courage.

Courage to Lead

Bill Hybels, lead pastor of Willow Creek Church just outside of Chicago, one of the largest churches in America, discovered the kind of people who lead what he called "prevailing churches."

> I shouldn't have been surprised that behind the scenes of every prevailing ministry I discovered courageous, servant-oriented leaders. Throughout history, whenever God was ready to begin a new work, he would tap a potential leader on the shoulder and give him or her a leadership assignment.[4]

Leadership is all about courage. I have discovered that most leaders can be divided into two categories. You might try to guess what those two categories are: gifted or not gifted; visionary or not visionary; high capacity or low capacity, etc. I think all these are valid leadership categories. But, the categories I'm talking about are *discouraged* and *encouraged*. I believe the dividing line in leadership effectiveness rests in one word: courage.

The discouraged leader is: passive, isolated, depressed, fearful, indecisive, anxious, tired, and has a difficult time living in a dynamic relationship with God themselves, much less leading other people to run hard after the heart of God.

The encouraged leader is: passionate, infectious, visionary, decisive, inspirational, highly motivated, and has lots of fun leading people to lay everything on the line for the global glory of God.

LifePoint Church (FBC, Smyrna at the time) could not possibly comprehend the courage it would take to become a Sending Church, but we were about to find out. Real courage can only come from God. So the depth of our connection with Him is vital to having courage to lead the church to *be* the church.

More than three hundred times in the Bible, God commands His people to "Fear not" or "Do not be afraid." Obviously, people courageous enough to step into the ring and do battle for the global glory of God will have to face off with the giants of fear, intimidation, and anxiety.

Joshua succeeded Moses as leader of God's people, Israel. During his commissioning and installation, God gave him specific words that would prove invaluable to his leadership. The entire theme in Joshua chapter 1 is "Courage." I think it's interesting that God didn't suggest that Joshua should be courageous; God *commanded* him to be courageous:

> Have I not commanded you? Be strong and courageous. Do not be frightened, and do not be dismayed, for the LORD your God is with you wherever you go. (Josh. 1:9)

My intent in writing this book is to encourage pastors and church leaders, but I also want to challenge you to be courageous because discouragement is not an option. Courage is a command, not a suggestion.

I offer this challenge because fear and discouragement are two of Satan's most effective tools. It's not "if" you face fear and discouragement; it's "when." I know that by experience and I bet you do too.

God knew Joshua's greatest leadership challenge would be to keep his courage. Formidable enemies—both within his own camp, as well as outside his camp—would challenge him every day. Through those enemies, all Satan had to do was to take Joshua's courage away and he would stop leading, dreaming, and obeying God.

Defining Moments

When I arrived in Smyrna, Ken was in his early sixties and he quickly became like a father to me. We had an Elijah/Elisha type of relationship (more on that later). He'd been a pastor and missionary for more than forty years and had fought more battles than Churchill and Patton combined.

The opportunity to work with Ken was what really compelled me to come to FBC, Smyrna. I knew I would be a pastor one day and wanted someone who had taken a few snaps to teach me how to throw the ball. So, I jumped at the opportunity to be mentored by such a wise and courageous leader.

One night, in the middle of the growing storm over the changes being made, two deacons knocked on Ken's door. One was in his mid-thirties and the other in his mid-sixties. The older deacon had no clue what was about to happen.

As soon as Ken opened the door, things went south when the young deacon threatened to whip Ken's backside (he said it a little differently). Ken shocked everybody when, rather than backing down, he said, "You are all mouth and no action. Step on in and let's see whose 'donkey' gets kicked." Now, that's a courageous leader. That's the moment I knew that I couldn't leave this man to fight this battle alone.

But, even the strong have moments of weakness. One day, Ken came to our staff meeting and stated that we were going to turn down the volume and go back to the hymnal. He had received too many complaints and was concerned that we would lose too many people.

There were three of us in the room that day—Ron Alley, Ken Hubbard, and me. Saying it got a little heated is like saying hell is a little hot. When we finally called a cease-fire and came out for a break, our administrative assistants were hiding in the kitchen. They literally thought we were going to come to blows.

After our break, I said:

> Ken, I love you. You're the pastor and we're obviously going to follow your lead. But, I want you to think about something. You're going to

retire in a few years and you have a decision to make. Do you want to kick it into cruise control and take the easy road out or do you want to do what's best for the church and go out with your boots on charging the hill?

Ken didn't talk about it anymore until Sunday. That's when he stood in the pulpit and said:

> Some of you don't like what we're doing to reach and disciple people and make this church relevant to the next generation. You're only interested in your desires and preferences. Some of you have even threatened to leave if we don't change things back. Well, this is what we're going to do in order to reach people and make disciples. If you don't like it, fire me and I'll put on my Bermuda shorts and go to Florida and play shuffleboard.

My chin hit the back of the pew in front of me (we had pews at that time). I was so proud of him. Not many pastors would be that bold at his stage of ministry. But, Ken Hubbard's agenda wasn't pleasing people; it was pleasing God. He'll always be one of the best and most courageous leaders I've ever known because of his commitment to change the world rather than pacify people.

When Ken spoke those words, the auditorium became eerily silent. Time seemed to stand still. It was one of those moments that you look back on later and realize that it was a defining, make-or-break, do-or-die moment. After a few seconds, a single snicker broke the silence, and then the entire place erupted in laughter.

In his way, Ken set the course and clearly communicated where we were going. There was no turning back. Did some of those people who threatened to leave follow through with their threats? Sure they did. Did it hurt to see people leave? It always has and always will. Was it worth it? I guess it depends on your agenda.

I'm sure the countless people who've heard the effectual call of God and had the eternal trajectory of their life changed would say it was worth it. I'm sure the countless marriages that have been redeemed would say it was worth it. I'm sure the countless grandparents who prayed continually for the salvation of their grandkids would say it was worth it. What do you think?

Your church is probably facing some kind of transition. I hope, by reading this, you realize that change is never easy. Leading a church to stay on task in its mission for the global glory of God will always take courageous leadership. There are no shortcuts in doing God's will.

Fast-Forward

After Ken's bold stand before the church, we began to grow so rapidly that we had to form a special growth committee to help us find possible solutions to park the cars and get butts in seats. Our auditorium was packed in two services, and every classroom was overflowing. Our staff gave up our offices and moved into a portable office so we would have more space for our preschoolers. We were literally turning people away because they had no room to park or sit. So, we decided to start a third service.

Preaching is the most important thing we pastors do and, if you're a pastor, you know how much preaching takes out of you. It is hard on a young man and, the older I get, the more I realize how brutal it is for an older man. Ken was already preaching two sermons and didn't think he could make it through another. So, he asked me if I would preach one of the three services and assume the role of Associate Pastor. I knew this was consistent with what God was leading me to do. So, even though it meant more responsibility with no more pay, I gladly jumped at the opportunity.

Before I arrived in Smyrna, Ken led the church to buy forty-four acres in a prime location on the loop that circles our community. At our current location, we were breaking every rule known to church growth experts.

Terrible parking, small restrooms, disastrous preschool and children's areas, hidden in a horrible location—these were just a few of our growth challenges. Yet, we had grown almost 100 percent in three years. So, we decided it was time to relocate the church. If you've ever tried to relocate a church, then you know that it might be easier to relocate the borders between Texas and Mexico.

A lot of very meaningful things happen in the buildings where churches meet. Daddies gave their daughters away in that building. Junior was baptized in that building. People met their husband or wife in that building. Grandparents were eulogized in that building. Excuse me, Mr. President, but until you've tried to relocate a church, "you ain't done nothing yet."

High Stakes

One day, while at a conference in Memphis, Ken and I were eating at a famous barbecue joint. Just as I was about to wrap my tongue around the most amazing baby back rib you could imagine, Ken said, "I've been talking to the deacons about you."

It was one of those moments where you have a hard decision to make: chomp down on the rib or put it down and slowly back away. I put the rib down and asked,

"What have you been talking to the deacon about?" He said, "They want to make you my co-pastor and put a succession plan in place for me to pass the baton to you when I retire." I thought these ribs must be soaked in some of Popcorn Sutton's best batch.

To be honest, in seminary it was a dream of mine to go to a church as the youth minister and, one day, become pastor and invest my life in one church. So, I couldn't believe what I was hearing. It was a dream, but I didn't really think it could become a reality.

I was so excited that I totally forgot about the ribs—it takes a lot to get me that excited. All of my excitement subsided when a thought hit me, *What does Ken think of this? If he doesn't like it, then I'll be looking for a job.* So, I swallowed and ask what he thought. He said:

> Son, nothing would make me happier. I fully believe you're the man for the job. So, unless you have any objections, I'm going to get the ball rolling.

The church had just voted to build a four-million-dollar building and relocate to our new property. Now, they were going to be asked to vote for me to be their new pastor who would succeed Ken. How many times has that happened effectively in a church?

I had mixed emotions. I was extremely excited and, at the same time, extremely nervous because it was a huge risk. By this time, we had about two hundred and fifty active students in our ministry. We were baptizing about seventy-five students a year. I was preaching every week and we were growing rapidly. I had a great relationship with the church and a great ministry. Things were great but, if the vote didn't go well, the awkwardness would be so crazy, I'd have to leave. But, it was a risk worth taking because we were confident it was God's direction.

The next few months weren't easy. You can't lead an organization for three years without making some people mad. Some would have given me their kidney and others wanted to cut out my heart. So, I spent many sleepless nights worrying about the vote . . . all for nothing. When the vote was finally taken, it was 98 percent positive.

This wasn't the end of the challenges; it was only the beginning. We challenged our people to live for the global glory of God and that would require making costly shifts in how we approached the world outside our church. Three major shifts represented dozens of smaller and more costly shifts to transition LifePoint:

1. From Attractional to Missional—We would maintain excellence, but would be more concerned with the

mission of God, even if that meant becoming less attractive to church consumers.

2. From One Campus to Multicampus—We would decentralize in our local community and take the church to the people, as opposed to waiting for the people to come to church.

3. From Local to "Glocal"—We would rename and reidentify ourselves in order to clearly identify and decentralize our mission worldwide.

Through this book, you'll read about these shifts and the challenges we faced to make them. Although the timing and details may look different in your context, the principle is the same: You must make costly changes to fulfill God's mission, and to make those changes you will need courage and a clear word from God.

LifePoint Church is 102 years old. Most churches this age are either already in the grave or someone is standing by with a shovel ready to start digging. But, there are a few that are just starting to hit their stride.

I believe the churches that are still kicking strong are the ones who are led by pastors like Ken Hubbard. Courageous pastors who:

- *value* making God famous, more than making people happy.

- *listen* to God's voice, rather than the voice of their critics.
- *preach* God's Word faithfully, no matter who it offends.
- *follow* the direction of God for the church, no matter who goes with him.

Churches that are changing the world also have courageous lay leaders who:

- *hold up* the pastor's hands in battle.
- *speak up* and tell self-centered critics to shut up.
- *stay* when it's so easy to leave.
- *lose* friends in order to gain the joy of living for the glory of God.

So, the question is, do you want to play church the rest of your life or do you want to change the world?

✝ *LifePoints . . .*

When you see what needs to be done, even though no one else sees it, and you know this is the direction that God wants you to go, you have to go . . . if you know it's what needs to be done and you don't do it, you are being disobedient. One of the reasons that God's hand has been on LifePoint is because the leadership has been willing to take us where we needed to go, whether it was easy or not. **—Milt**

~~~~~~

Some Christians want to attend church on Sundays and Wednesdays and hear how to be a better Christian. They want to work on themselves not others. Those who want to live comfortable lives do not like that we are so focused on sending. **—Erica**

~~~~~~

I believe the biggest challenge that LifePoint faced was on our pastor's shoulders to cast a clear and powerful vision to our people. Then the pastor and staff had to continually recast and recommunicate that vision over and over so that now it is the heartbeat of our church! **—Brittany**

Moving Forward . . .

1. What is the greatest hindrance to the gospel in your community?

2. How would your community change if that hindrance was removed?

Chapter 3

More

*When they had crossed, Elijah said to Elisha,
"Ask what I shall do for you, before I am taken
from you." And Elisha said, "Please let there
be a double portion of your spirit on me."*

(2 Kings 2:9)

ROB AND CYNTHI LAW were living the high life. But that was before the tornado struck Murfreesboro, Tennessee, on Good Friday in 2009. The Law household wasn't physically affected by that tornado, but their lives were wrecked all the same.

While Rob worked with a disaster relief team to help a man clean up years of accumulated stuff, a really nice flat-screen TV caught his attention. Rob had an identical flat-screen TV at home, but there was one major difference; this flat screen had a huge hole in the middle. However, this man's spirit was infectious. He told Rob, "This is just stuff. My people are OK and that's all that matters."

God used that experience to knock Rob and Cynthi off center and cause them to be dissatisfied with life as usual. In spite of becoming incredibly successful, Rob knew there had to be more. Rob had been a Christ follower for several years and was serious about his faith. But that nagging feeling wouldn't go away. The hole in the flat screen was stuck in his head. All that man had was scattered over the front yard like confetti at a Super Bowl parade, but it didn't seem to bother him. Rob was captured by the reality that stuff is just stuff.

That day, God made it clear to Rob that there was more to life than chasing after position or possessions. In a matter of seconds, all your "stuff" can be ripped to pieces and scattered like dust in the wind. Rob knew he could no longer invest his life in temporal things. He knew it was time to invest his life in something that lasts forever.

So, Rob and Cynthi began downsizing. The first thing to go was their Lincoln Navigator. Then, Rob sold his PSLs (personal seat licenses) for his Tennessee Titans' season tickets. OK, even I began to think he was overdoing it just a bit. Getting rid of a Navigator is one thing, but getting rid of NFL tickets . . . let's not get too carried away.

Rob's goal was to live light and become mobile so he would be ready to go wherever or do whatever God directed him to do. Three years later, Rob, Cynthi, and their three children are living in our mission house preparing to move to Brussels. Rob will work in the marketplace to develop relationships and build influence for the kingdom.

His Leaders Are Temporary

A few years ago, getting a job in another country with the intention of building relationships to share the gospel and plant churches wasn't on the radar of LifePointers. But, today, it's as much a part of the LifePoint culture as our Sunday morning gatherings.

Chaos in the form of radical change has become a way of life for us now. We continually see people set free from bondage to the mundane world of punching a clock as their job becomes more than a payday; it becomes their mission field. We see people begin to live for passion rather than possession as they sell out to move to another culture to share the gospel and plant churches. Like a tornado, God blew through our church in 2004, totally destroying many things that we held tight and thought were important.

We still have issues and problems, what church doesn't? But they're nothing like the old issues and problems that used to drive me crazy—like people getting upset because we changed something that Grandma did when she was a kid, or because the music is too loud, or the preacher is wearing jeans on the stage.

Those issues matter very little now. What matters is the gospel and the fact that two-thirds of the world has never even met a Christian, much less heard one explain the gospel.

Two years after we moved into our new building, Ken announced his retirement. We know that God ordains all things from beginning to end, but it became crazy obvious how God had ordained my relationship with Ken Hubbard and the succession plan for FBC, Smyrna.

Can you imagine how difficult it would be for a growing church to relocate and build a new building in a new location and then have their pastor retire? But, because of God's sovereign plan, rather than losing momentum, we actually picked up steam.

Ken's retirement celebration was an amazing tribute to an amazing man and an incredible leader. Laughter was loud and tears were rolling. The night was full of stories from people who had been greatly affected by his fifty years of dynamic ministry.

Ken was famous for wearing a white suit and white buck suede shoes every Easter. This was one of his trademarks that everyone thought was hilarious, but no one dared joke about . . . until I arrived. I couldn't help it . . . he practically painted a target on his chest and asked me to take a shot. All it took was one joke to free everyone up to get in on the action.

I asked Faye, Ken's wife, to secretly bring me his famous white suit for the retirement celebration. We rigged it in a way that would allow it to slowly descend into the center of the auditorium.

When Ken stepped to the podium, we turned the lights down and the music up. It was the music that you hear in an NBA basketball arena when the home team is introduced. All of a sudden, the white suit was hit with a spot light and began to slowly descend from the middle of the auditorium. Yes, we were retiring the white suit. Everybody loved it!

A few weeks later, Ken preached his last sermon and it was unforgettable. The place was packed with people who had come to celebrate the retirement of a legend. When he walked on stage that morning, he was wearing a red sash around his neck that hung down to below his waist. As you've probably already guessed, his last message was about Elijah passing his mantle to his protégé, Elisha.

The more I think back, the more I realize that Ken was a genius, and a great case study in leadership. Many pastors find it hard to let go. Generally, three groups of people hang on way too long: politicians, athletes, and preachers. They just can't seem to step out of the spotlight. But, Ken's passion wasn't his kingdom; it was God's kingdom. His desire wasn't to leave a memory; it was to leave a legacy.

Ken was an incredible friend and an awesome mentor who intentionally groomed me to be the lead pastor of LifePoint Church. He understood that I would lead in a totally different world and in a totally different style than he did. So he did not make his methods holy or let them become a golden calf for people to worship.

I hope I can follow Ken's example. One day, sooner than I want to imagine, a new man will lead LifePoint. At that time, even though I hope to still be on the cutting edge, I'm sure many of our methods will seem old and outdated to the new generation. Like milk, our methods may be fresh today, but if we keep hanging on to them, they'll quickly go sour. That will be the true test of my leadership. Like Ken, I want to finish well for the glory of God and future generations.

Ken's message about Elijah and Elisha was spot-on. You can read the incredible leadership story in 1 Kings 19–2 Kings 2. You will find that God had a succession plan in place. Why? Because His mission is sacred, His glory is magnificent, and His leaders are all temporary.

Passing the Mantle

Elijah was in the midst of deep depression. He felt alone and knew the evil Jezebel was about to make him the last casualty in God's army. At his deepest point of struggle, God showed him the plan. He told Elijah that Elisha would be the one, "you shall anoint to be prophet in your place" (1 Kings 19:16).

God's succession plan was in place for Elijah. I think the story provides a great model for the church to follow. Few are willing to entertain that thought, but we should. I'm so grateful that I was blessed to learn from a selfless servant-leader who died to self to make Jesus famous.

The term *servant-leader* doesn't even make sense from the world's point of view. How can a servant be a leader?

How can a leader be a servant? Does being a servant-leader mean you let people run over you? Hardly!

Jesus was the most amazing servant-leader in history. We read about Him standing up to the most intimidating people in the first century, the Jewish religious leaders. We read about Him flipping over tables and chasing people out of town with a bullwhip. I don't think that would be classified as weak or wimpy. A servant-leader leads, not with his best interests in mind, but with the best interests of God's kingdom in mind. This is exactly what Ken did, and God has been highly exalted as a result of his humility.

At the end of his sermon, Ken walked over to me and asked me to stand. I was a little nervous, not knowing what to expect. He looked me in the eye and smiled and then removed the mantle (based on the leadership principle in 2 Kings 2) from around his neck and placed it around my neck and said:

> I'm passing my mantle to my Elisha. Pat Hood is now my pastor. I will follow where he leads this church. Don't ever let me hear you be critical of or complain about my pastor. I won't stand for it. I love him, I trust him, and I will follow him.

The church stood and applauded, and there wasn't a dry eye in the house. Talk about finishing strong!

After Ken retired, we started the process of hiring an Executive Pastor to lead our staff. There was only one person for the job—Kyle Goen. Kyle had left Florida and was now serving as the Executive Pastor of a large church in a wealthy suburb of Houston, Texas. I knew Kyle was making more money than we could ever pay, but I wasn't going to give up. I hoped he loved me more than the "Benjamins." At least that was the card I was going to play.

When I called Kyle, he wasn't shocked because we had dreamed about this for years. But, the fact that it was actually happening was still a little overwhelming. Kyle had told his pastor in Texas that I was the only other pastor he would consider serving with. Now, it was time to test his resolve.

Leaving Texas was not an easy decision for Kyle. He loved me, but he also loved his pastor in Texas. His kids were young and he was making A LOT more money than we could offer. I even asked our committee to consider paying Kyle more than me because I knew how critical his leadership would be in helping navigate the route God was directing us to take.

The committee wouldn't agree to paying him more than me because, at the time, we were still governed by the same constitution and bylaws as practically every small Baptist church in America. Every staff salary was made public for everyone to see and discuss during the monthly business meeting.

The committee knew that the Executive Pastor making more than the Senior Pastor would go over like a pregnant pole vaulter, but they did agree to offer him just a little less than me. But, in the end, the money really didn't matter. Kyle knew that God had ordained this before time began. So, he packed up and moved his family to Smyrna in 2002. Little did we know, the fun was just beginning.

Becoming a Sending Church

I've always been a pastor who loves people and loves seeing their lives transformed by Jesus. But, admittedly, there was a time when I was more concerned with growing the church than sending the church. Sadly, I was focused on the wrong scorecard.

Here's a principle every pastor should consider:

> To be truly successful, you must keep score on the right scorecard.

According to our old scorecard, we were knocking it out of the park. We were reaching a lot of unchurched people, receiving record offerings, and baptizing more people than ever. We thought we were headed for the pinnacle of success with a new building and bigger crowds. Everything seemed to be going right, but I knew in my heart that something was desperately wrong.

Every church keeps score. Every church measures progress. The scorecard that most pastors and churches use revolves around what we commonly call the three Bs: butts, buildings, and budgets. If you're getting more butts in seats and more money in the budget and planning to build bigger buildings, then you're usually considered very "successful" in the church world. The problem is when our definition of "success" isn't God's definition of success.

Don't misunderstand, numbers are very important at LifePoint. We count the number of people in our weekly worship gatherings. We count the number of people in small groups. We count our money. We set goals to increase attendance, giving, small group participation, and serving. So, don't think I'm saying keeping score isn't spiritual. My intent is to help you understand that numbers don't tell the whole story nor do they necessarily measure success. As a matter of fact, if winning is all about getting more people, more money, and building bigger, cooler buildings, then you're never going to win because butts, budgets, and buildings are all moving targets.

Oh, you can do some really "good" stuff. You can attract a large crowd and maybe even make the list of the one hundred fastest growing churches in America. You can build some really big and really cool buildings. You can collect more money than the IRS . . . well, maybe not. But, you can have all these "wins" and still lose if that is your end game, because success on God's scorecard isn't just about buildings, butts, and budgets.

God measures obedience rather than bigness.

Rather than measuring the size of our buildings or the size of our attendance, God measures the size of our passion to run hard after His heart and His purpose for the church.

Leading a Sending Church is the most fun I've ever had—but, don't think it has been all cookies and Kool-Aid. It has also been one of the most intense challenges I've ever faced. If you desire to lead your church to follow the direction of God rather than the whims of people, you will experience more challenges than a woman trying to become the president of Iran—that, I can guarantee.

If the mission of Satan is to keep lost people lost, who do you think is going to intimidate him more . . . a "successful" church whose mission is to play it safe, attract large crowds, and build bigger buildings? . . . or a church that is courageous enough to become a Sending Church, that deploys missionaries to the football fields, businesses, schools, and neighborhoods—that shares the gospel and plants churches, both in our communities and around the world?

When I look back at the story of how God brought LifePoint to where we are today, I see specific challenges we experienced. And, although we're light-years ahead of where we were in 2000, we still take a step back every now and then. At times sending gives way to struggling. At other times, we revert back to the old scorecard because it is so easy to feel good about what's going on if it can be tangibly measured in buildings, budgets, or butts.

Here is an overview of the challenging phases we had to move through in order to become a Sending Church:

Struggle: Everything is a battle during this phase because people are more concerned about their desires and preferences than in the heart of God or the eternal destinies of people. Making changes that will help you become more effective in reaching people outside the church is sometimes like asking people to sell their firstborn child. People really don't want to be challenged; they want to be pampered. People get upset if someone sits in the seat they've always sat in. You often find yourself managing the emotional whims of people—like what makes them happy, what makes them angry, and what hurts their feelings. People complain about the pastor caring more for those outside the church than those we already have. The church is internally focused rather than externally focused. You look out the window and wonder why you're here and quietly wish you were somewhere else.

Success: You've been bold enough to stay in the battle. As a result, you start reaching new people. The parking lot starts filling up and there is life in the church. You put on the waders and get in the baptistery almost every week. New leaders begin to emerge. The offerings are getting better and better. You start talking about building space to reach even more people. You hire more staff. Momentum is building. The preaching even seems to be better.

Significance or Satisfaction: It's a new day and things are going great. Your church is creating a buzz all over town. Word of mouth suddenly positions your church as the Sunday place to be. Lives are being changed and marriages are being redeemed. People are actually excited about inviting their neighbors, friends, and work associates to church gatherings. Your peers begin to notice that your church is making a difference and are even starting to ask "How to" questions. There are fewer battles over the preferences of people. People are satisfied and you should be too, except for the fact that something is stirring and you are privately disappointed that significance and "success" does not feel better than it does.

Sending: A growing restlessness with significance, satisfaction, and "success" finally brings you to a place where God can take over. At this point things really get crazy. The cycle seems to go back to the beginning—to the struggle phase. Although the struggles are different, they are tougher than ever. God begins to radically transform the hearts and ambitions of you and your people. People in your church begin to see their jobs as their mission field. Some even quit their jobs, sell their possessions, and move to another culture to share the gospel. Your best friends may even feel God directing them to pack up and move to another country for the sake of the gospel.

You keep score differently now. It's not just about the number of people who come to your building; it's about the number of people being sent out of the building on mission in the community and around the world.

Missions is no longer a department in your church; it's what we give our lives, our money, and our time to, so that lost people can worship God. Suddenly, your people realize salvation isn't about them; it's about the global glory of God. Members are becoming global Christians who care as much about those on the other side of the world as they do about your local community. Your people don't just see missions as a "trip," they see missions as life. Missions isn't "vacational" (something they take a week off work to do), it's "vocational" (it's what their life is about).

These are some of the phases that we progressed through on our way to becoming a Sending Church. And, I believe, any church that sets out to hear the voice of God, and adjusts accordingly, will experience similar challenges.

Managing a church can be comfortable and safe, but leading a church is messy and dangerous. Don't picture it as a conveyor belt on an assembly line; think of it as a washing machine agitator. The key word here is *agitator.*

In this analogy, the global glory of God is the agitator and the tub is the local church. The agitator constantly keeps stirring and vibrating the contents in the tub to knock off the dirt that spoils the garments—the dirt of consumer Christianity, the dirt of "success," the dirt of religion, the dirt of being safe and comfortable.

Please, don't fall for the lie that pursuing the heart of God makes things smooth and easy. It's just the opposite. The church that runs hard after the heart and mission of God will be a church that experiences an ongoing purification process of becoming more like Jesus.

If we really want to impact our world, then we must become totally dependent upon the power of God. We can't change our church. We can change our music, our paint, and our dress. We can even change our culture, but we can't change our church . . . only God can do that.

So, my confidence is not, nor has it ever been, in people, including myself. We have been utterly depraved and deeply flawed since Genesis 3. My confidence is in the One who spoke the world into existence, parted the Red Sea, and brings dead men and women back to life.

✝ *LifePoints . . .*

I have a constant gnawing at my heart to "go." I wrestle daily with the Holy Spirit to understand what I am supposed to do. He wants more from me. He wants everything I have. Before LifePoint, I was satisfied in my walk with Jesus, but now I am beginning (although it is still very childlike) to actually see the world as Christ sees it. *—Doug*

~~~~~~~~

The people of LifePoint are real. We struggle, we fail, but we also seek after the real redemption of Christ together. There are no pretentions at LifePoint. This transparency has made my own faith stronger, richer, and more authentic. *—Amy*

~~~~~~~~

My personal experience with the Bangkok mission team has allowed me to see spiritual struggle and change in Thai lives. We have a young chemical engineer who is the only believer in his family. He now feels called to pastor his people. I think this shows how LifePoint's goal isn't to "convert," but rather make disciples and empower leaders. *—Seth*

Moving Forward . . .

1. When in your life were you the closest to God?

2. How can you retrace your steps and return to that place?

Chapter 4

If You Build It, They Will Come

So then you are no longer strangers and aliens, but you are fellow citizens with the saints and members of the household of God, built on the foundation of the apostles and prophets, Christ Jesus himself being the cornerstone, in whom the whole structure, being joined together, grows into a holy temple in the Lord. In him you also are being built together into a dwelling place for God by the Spirit.

(EPHESIANS 2:19–22)

IN THE MOVIE *FIELD of Dreams*, Kevin Costner played the role of an Iowa farmer who felt a mystical urge to build a baseball field on his farm. When he built the field, ghosts from the 1919 Chicago Black Sox appeared, walking out of his cornfield. The famous voice heard by Costner's character in the movie repeated, "If you build it, they will come."

Pastors seem to have that same mystical urge to build things in hopes that people will appear out of thin air. I must admit that there was a time when I believed that voice too. So have many of you.

LifePoint was preparing to open a new auditorium so more people could "come." The three Bs on our scorecard were tracking well. We were about to reach what most of us felt was the summit of success. But, as Jim Collins said in his hit business book, *Good to Great*, we almost missed something great to settle for something we thought was "good."

Right-Sizing the Gorilla

Mike Miller, President of NavPress, is a good friend and was a VP at LifeWay Christian Resources at the time. He was working with us in a consulting role to help us formalize our future vision.

Ken had just retired and Kyle Goen was about to begin serving as my Executive Pastor. I wanted Kyle to hit the ground running. So, before he officially started, I flew him in to meet with Mike and me about some changes we were going to implement over the next year.

One of those changes would be our staff structure. Before, our staff structure was flat-lined. There was basically a direct line from me to every staff member. Mike helped me to see how unhealthy this was for both the church and me. So, to be more efficient and effective, Kyle was going to lead and supervise the staff.

I called an "all staff" meeting to share our new organizational structure. I introduced Kyle and said, "I hope you like this guy because he's your new boss." We outlined how everything would work and I thought everything went well. But, I was wrong.

To say my staff was shocked would be an understatement. They loved answering directly to me and didn't want to change. Change is a required ingredient for growth, but that doesn't make it easy. So, there was some unexpected pushback and, in the end, some weren't willing to make the sacrificial changes. But, it was one of the best organizational moves we've ever made.

I didn't realize how much time I spent dealing with issues that I didn't need to be involved with. This structure change gave me the bandwidth to do what only I could do—lead, preach, and cast vision for the church.

We had grown from five hundred to almost fifteen hundred without a single change to our structure. Committee approval, deacon approval, and congregational approval in the monthly business meeting was required before any plan could be implemented. Our staff could make no real decisions without the approval of committees, deacons, and the church. It took at least a month to decide if we were going to install black or brown mulch in the landscaping. Obviously, this created an enormous drag on the church that created a lot of tension and inefficiency.

For example, after studying our growth challenges, our staff felt we needed to change our corporate worship times to provide more time between gatherings. This would open more parking spaces for later services and give our next-generation ministries more time to turn over the environment between services. The move was a no-brainer if our objective was to reach more people.

But some people didn't want to make these changes. The new times would totally mess up Sunday morning routines. So, the prevailing thought wasn't how changing times would help us reach lost people; the only consideration was how it affected "me." So, many wanted to vote on it.

I remember being so frustrated in a meeting that I finally said,

> Look, there are some things we're going to vote on and others we're not going to vote on. You hired me to lead this church and be your pastor. If you don't want me to lead; just tell me and I'll go somewhere else.

This is purely description, not prescription. I really don't suggest you try this. Although I left this meeting with all my limbs intact, it wasn't the smartest thing I've ever done. I had a lot of change in my pocket and, to be honest, I was young and a little arrogant.

Leading doesn't mean shoving authority in someone's face or making sure people know who's in charge; leading is influence and I could have used my influence a little better in this case.

As I mentioned in chapter 1, monthly business meetings were frustrating in the old structure. They gave the church a forum for members to disagree over insignificant issues. I firmly believe there are a few things a church should vote on . . . but not many. We needed a new structure to support the work God was going to call us to do.

Growing Restlessness

We had grown about 300 percent in six years. We were seeing more people baptized than ever and we were collecting record offerings. This is what most churches pray for and most pastors dream about. You'd think every member of LifePoint would be smiling like a man on his honeymoon. But, many looked like they were having a root canal with a power drill.

People had prayed for a renewed and revitalized church for years and now they were living it. But rather than being grateful, they were uncomfortable. People were being transformed by the grace of God. Families were being saved. Teenagers were making God famous in their schools. Yet, instead of celebrating, many were sad because of the methods we were using and their perceived loss of control.

Sunday became a weird experience. I'd walk down the hallway and see people who had just been baptized and they were so excited about their new faith. I'd look in the other direction and see a husband and wife whose marriage had one foot in the grave, but just like Lazarus, Jesus brought it back from the dead. I'd see so many new faces and shake the hands of so many guests.

Then, I'd turn a corner and see a group of people huddled up murmuring about the loud music or our attempt to start small groups on Sunday night or . . . you fill in the preference. Two different churches existed in one building. And like riding a roller coaster, I was on top of the peak one minute and plunging into the valley the next.

I was a young pastor who took everything personal. Every negative comment or harsh word cut straight to my heart like a surgeon's scalpel. I read every negative e-mail and then read it again in my mind as I laid my head on my pillow. These were the most exciting and most difficult days I've ever experienced.

I loved seeing people's lives changed and, at the same time, I hated seeing people care more about the style of music or the dress code than the heart of God. I loved seeing new Christians, still wet behind the ears, excited about their new faith. But I hated seeing longtime church members miserable because someone was sitting in the seat they occupied for years. I loved seeing newborn Christians and hated seeing people who had claimed Jesus for years still acting like a newborn Christian.

Many Christians talk a good game when it comes to obeying the Great Commission, but few really want to do what it takes. They celebrate missionaries going to Africa, dressing like the Africans, using African music, speaking African languages, and meeting in African buildings to reach African people. But if people in our city want to hear about Jesus, they need to come to us on our terms, listen to our music, dress like we dress, and learn our language.

As ridiculous as it sounds, this is the picture of many, if not most, churches in America today. Does it really surprise us that thousands of churches close their doors every year?

Finding a Structure That Works

Our structure needed a major overhaul. We had created our own political system that entitled every church member to express their opinions and vote on insignificant issues. Leadership in the church was nothing more than a popularity contest because it was done by popular vote. This needed to change. Gifts, passions, abilities, and spiritual fruit should be the criteria for leadership, not just church membership.

So, we undertook the task of changing our governing documents to allow people who actually knew something about finances and obeyed God with the tithe to make financial decisions. We wanted people who actually worked in human resources to make personnel decisions. We wanted people who had proven their faith with the fruit of their life to make the decisions.

Our change management committee worked hard for many long months to produce a constitution and bylaws (CBL) that we felt allowed us to be more effective and efficient by giving the staff high freedom and high accountability.

To say the new CBL was a radical shift from our previous structure would be like calling the Grand Canyon a ditch. We downsized to only three committees of seven people each; the personnel, stewardship, and business process committees. Those twenty-one people, plus myself, became the board of directors who were given authority to make decisions for the church. The church would only have one annual business meeting in November to approve the budget and vote on the new board members, who would make decisions and do business on behalf of the church.

You would have thought we had just laid out the Communist Manifesto. I literally can't believe I made it through this time. When the proposed CBL was presented for the first reading, one man immediately tried to bring confusion by standing up and declaring that the Bible teaches that deacons should control all the money in the church. After the meeting, I approached him and put my hand on his shoulder and explained that the statements he made were false teaching and if it happened again, I would be forced to call him out publicly for teaching false doctrine.

The next Sunday, I had an incredible young leader stop by my office. He awkwardly said, "Pat, I need to ask you one question and whatever you say is good enough for me." I thought it was a little strange, but said, "OK, shoot."

He asked, "Did you get Bob (that's what we'll call him) in a headlock Wednesday night after church?" I thought it was joke, so I laughed. But he was dead serious. I said, "No, I didn't, but I sure would have liked too." I found out later that rumors were flying that I had gotten Bob in a headlock and threatened him if he ever spoke against our new CBL again. Someone must have read my mind.

I'm grateful for the leaders who rode like mighty warriors beside, behind, and out in front of me during this time. LifePoint wouldn't be where it is today without strong and courageous leaders, who support, encourage, challenge, and protect the pastor. I learned through this, the last thing the church needs is weak leaders.

When it came time to vote on our new CBL, people showed up that I'd never seen before. I was told that some of the detractors had their teenagers bring friends to vote "no." In the end, the new CBL failed by less than ten votes. I was more than frustrated.

Within a few minutes, our entire staff and their spouses filled my office. They were looking to me for a word of encouragement. I told them I didn't have any encouraging words, but I wasn't willing to continue under the old, ineffective system that distracted people from God's mission. I was tired of fighting the battles required to simply buy a box of ink pens.

I'll never forget, with tears in his eyes, Kyle spoke up and said, "I'm called to serve alongside you. Whatever you decide is what we'll do."

The next Sunday, I brought the entire staff up to the front of the auditorium after each gathering and told the congregation that one of the most important votes in the history of our church had failed by less than ten votes. But, I assured them this wasn't the end of the race. It was just a hurdle we had to get over. Nothing worth anything comes easy. I promised that we were coming back at it again because God has called us to impact the world and we were committed to getting the job done.

I really didn't know how the church would respond. So, I was blown away when 90 percent of the people stood to their feet and applauded. At that moment the people who opposed the new governing structure realized that they had won the battle, but lost the war.

God's Faithfulness in the Midst of Pressure

We relocated to our new property in April of 1998. By 2002, we were already out of space again. So, we entered into another financial campaign to raise the money to build a new fifteen-hundred-seat auditorium.

We had just completed our campaign and had broken ground on our new building when the vote on our CBL was taken. As I think back, I realize how crazy that sounds. We were voting to spend several million dollars, building a new auditorium and adopt a new CBL within a few months of each other. Maybe that was too big of a bite to ask the church to chew at once, but we were growing so fast we didn't want to get further behind.

Then, in the fall of 2003, about three hundred people who opposed the new governing structure and disliked our methods and strategy, decided to go start a new traditional church. It wasn't mean or ugly. Most of those people love me and I love them. We just had two different agendas and two different interpretations of the mission of the church.

Just because it wasn't ugly, doesn't mean it wasn't painful. We were in the middle of trying to raise the money to pay for the new building that was already coming out of the ground. So, obviously, I was more than a little stressed. I believed with all my heart that God would provide the resources to fund His vision. But, in all honesty, it still kept me awake at night worrying about how we would be affected financially and numerically.

We were averaging more than fifteen hundred in attendance at the time. So losing three hundred would take us down to at least twelve hundred. I wondered how many other people would get wounded by friendly fire and sucked out in the draft. I feared that, in the end, we might lose as many as five hundred people.

Obviously, it was a tense time. But I was blown away by God's faithfulness. All of a sudden, Sunday mornings weren't weird or stressful. The negativity in the hallway ceased. The tension was gone. It was like someone had hit the pressure release button.

As a result, we saw immediate growth. Within a few months, we were back over fifteen hundred. We hardly noticed the dip in our giving and, by the next year, we received 104 percent of our budget. I learned a valuable lesson through this experience: don't be afraid that losing people means losing their money because, most of the time, people's money leaves a long time before they do.

Where Does God Dwell?

Two perspectives keep the "If you build it" movement alive. The first perspective comes from past success. There was a day in America where church was on people's radar. Most people went to church with their families in most communities, especially in the South. I am not so convinced we were building great disciples for Jesus, but we were drawing crowds.

The fifties, sixties, and seventies were years of unprecedented numerical growth in church attendance. Since that time we have witnessed the megachurch (two thousand attendees or more) and the gigachurch (ten thousand or more) phenomenon. Yet in the midst of mass warehouses of Christians, America has never been less Christian. Migration to the next big Christian show in town has created a generation of church consumers indifferent to the fact that people die without Christ in their communities every day.

Past success has played a role in sabotaging the mission of God, but that is not all. The second perspective of the "If you build it" movement is an Old Testament theology of church. I am not suggesting that people are using OT Bible verses to defend an attractional approach to church. Satan is way too subtle for that. I am saying that an ancient view of the temple—that says God only dwells in a geographical place—continues to influence the mind-set of many people in the church today, and they don't even realize it. The results are devastating for the mission of God.

For a great perspective on this, I suggest you read 1 Kings 8. It tells the story of the grand opening of the first temple. As the Israelites had spent years wondering in the wilderness because of their disobedience and lack of trust, God had told them to build a portable tabernacle for His symbolic presence to dwell among the people.

God couldn't dwell in the lives of His people because their sin had not yet been atoned for by the sacrifice of Jesus on the cross. So, instead of indwelling His people, God's presence dwelled symbolically among them in a place located in the innermost part of the tabernacle called the Holy of Holies.

After Israel was established and at peace, King David realized that he had built a beautiful city and was living in a blinged-out mansion while God was living in a tent in the backyard. David knew something was definitely wrong with this picture. So, he decided to build God a massive, multibillion-dollar temple. But God had other plans.

God told David his history was filled with too much bloodshed to build the temple. Instead, God told David that his son, Solomon, would lead the construction project.

David's response is amazing. He didn't pout or sulk. He simply said, "If I can't build it, I'll finance it so people I'll never even meet can worship God." I call that a mature believer, a legacy builder. That's seeing the big picture.

David was mature enough to realize that the temple wasn't about his kingdom or his name; it was about God's kingdom and God's name. So, he said, "If I can't do it, I'll fund it." If a church had one hundred people with this attitude, vision, and level of maturity, the community and the world would stand up and take notice.

Awesome Buildings

The new Cowboys' Stadium in Dallas cost around 1.3 billion dollars and took almost four years to build. It's the largest domed stadium in the world and has TV screens that stretch from 20-yard-line to 20-yard-line, that's 60 yards of screen for your viewing pleasure. But, the stadium sits relatively empty most of the time. Cowboys' fans meet there to worship their beloved Cowboys eight times a year, maybe nine if they make the playoffs.

In comparison, some estimate that Solomon's temple cost about 14 billion dollars in today's economy. It took seven years to build and, as much as I love football, it was for a much greater cause. Solomon spared no expense because this place would bear God's name and promote His greatness.

Back to 1 Kings 8: When the temple was complete, the priests carefully moved the ark of the covenant into the Holy of Holies. The ark of the covenant was the box that contained the Ten Commandments.

Only the high priest could enter the Holy of Holies one day a year, on the Day of Atonement (Yom Kippur), where he would make sacrifices for the sins of the people. The temple was amazing, but without the ark it was just another building. The ark was the symbol of God's presence and covenant with Israel. After the ark was placed in the Holy of Holies, things radically changed:

> And when the priests came out of the Holy Place, a cloud filled the house of the LORD, so the priests could not stand to minister because of the cloud, for the glory of the LORD filled the house of the LORD. (1 Kings 8:10–11)

The cloud symbolized the presence and glory of God. The same story in 2 Chronicles 7 tells us that fire fell from heaven when God's glory filled the temple. What an awesome thing to be in the presence of God!

The activity *of* God seems to be sadly missing from our activity *for* God today. Without the presence and power of God, we become just another social club or religious group. Much of our obsession with the local church buildings is an obsession with activity.

Whether we are meeting on the football field, riding motorcycles, or gathering together in large and small groups, God becomes the most craveable part of the meeting. God's people do not crave activity or busyness. They crave the living God. If we want God to be glorified in all we do, then we must embrace the necessity of His presence in all we do.

Solomon knew that God didn't actually live in the temple. God could never be contained in a geographic location. He knew that heaven can't even contain God, let alone a building. Listen as he prays:

> But will God indeed dwell on the earth? Behold, heaven and the highest heaven cannot contain you; how much less this house that I have built! (1 Kings 8:27)

Sending Churches are moved by the greatness of God and empowered and sent by Him to make His name great among the nations. They pray big prayers because they serve a big God who will save all who repent and call on Him.

But their view of God is not confined to a place, no matter how incredible that place might be. They are not waiting at a building for God and their neighbors to show up. The Sending Church has left the building.

God Dwells in a Person

The Bible contains 66 books, 1,189 chapters, and more than 31,100 verses, but it tells one story from beginning to end, the story of Jesus.

I generally don't like paraphrases. I'm partial to verse-by-verse translations like *The English Standard Version* or the *Holman Christian Standard Bible* because I think every word is critically important to God's revelation. But, I do like Eugene Peterson's paraphrase from John that captures the New Testament view of Jesus:

> The Word became flesh and blood, and moved into the neighborhood. We saw the glory with our own eyes, the one-of-a-kind glory, like Father, like Son, generous inside and out, true from start to finish. (John 1:14 *The Message*)

In the original language, the words translated "moved in" or "dwelled" in other versions, is the word *tabernacled*. God's presence was no longer in a place (tabernacle/temple), it was in a person, Jesus.

Jesus was God in the flesh who made His dwelling among us. He lived a sinless life and died our death to pay the price for our sin. As a result, He made it possible for God to live *in us* versus simply living *close to us*.

God Dwells in a People

After Jesus' death and resurrection, God now lives in the church. But, the church is not a building; it's a people. So, don't ever tell your kids they can't run or fight in God's house. This teaches them that God lives in a place and we go visit Him once or twice a week. Instead, teach them that God's house is the soul of every man, woman, boy, and girl who repents and surrenders to Jesus.

We're now living temples. God's presence and glory lives in us. If you take that lightly, then you don't understand true salvation. How can a believer who understands that the Holy Spirit indwells their life ever be satisfied with living a casual life driven by their own desires and ambitions? We're not perfect, but there's no way that someone who has the Spirit of God living within them can continually live a lifestyle contrary to the will of God.

Paul explained our responsibility as God's temples:

> Or do you not know that your body is a temple of the Holy Spirit within you, whom you have from God? You are not your own, for you were bought with a price. So glorify God in your body. (1 Cor. 6:19–20)

God lives in those who surrender to Him. He doesn't indwell His children for their benefit; He indwells us for His benefit. He invades our soul to empower us to live as sent people who represent Him in a hurting and hopeless world.

Sadly, through our language and structures, many churches still live an Old Testament theology that focuses on getting people to a building rather than sending people out of the building.

Our mission is to point people to a Christ-centered life and have a heart that burns hot for His fame. Pointing people to a building is not our mission, nor is it biblical. We want to point them to Jesus who will set them free from their bondage to sin, indwell their souls, and empower them to live as people sent into the world to represent His name.

⳨ *LifePoints . . .*

Change is generally not easy. But, if you are ever a part of something that only God can do and see His hand at work—if only for a moment—you will never, ever be satisfied with anything less! **—Kenny**

~~~~~

Without strong leadership devoted to God's plan, it's all pointless. So many obstacles were overcome because people were willing to stand up for what they believe in. Without people like that, LifePoint wouldn't be where it is today. It takes strong leadership and determination but most of all, complete reliance on God and His plan. **—Justin**

~~~~~

People from all ages at our church caught a vision for the future. Our seniors care more about the Kingdom and the future of the church than their own preferences. Some great, older leaders have championed the changes that have been made over the past fifteen years, even if it's not their favorite style of music, preaching, etc. **—Micah**

Moving Forward . . .

1. What is the toughest decision you are facing now in your ministry?

2. What do you need to help you make that decision?

Chapter 5

A Sacred Gathering

*Consecrate a fast; call a solemn assembly. Gather the
elders and all the inhabitants of the land to the house
of the LORD your God, and cry out to the LORD.*

(JOEL 1:14)

IN JANUARY 2004, I was having my morning quiet time.
I generally work, verse by verse, through a book of the
Bible. Some days I get through an entire chapter and some
days I only get through a verse. My objective isn't to check
another book off my list; my objective is for God's Word
to change me.

I was working my way through the book of Joel when
I came to Joel 1:14. I've read that verse so many times that

it had become familiar. And, when something is familiar, you tend to do a drive-by. It's like driving out of my neighborhood. A man could be running with nothing on but his sneakers and a smile and I probably wouldn't even notice. But this time was different. I felt the Holy Spirit compel me to pause and think about what I had just read. Did God want me to fast? Did He want me to call the church to fast?

The next day, I continued reading the book of Joel and came to Joel 2:15–16:

> Blow the trumpet in Zion; consecrate a fast; call a solemn assembly; gather the people. Consecrate the congregation; assemble the elders; gather the children, even nursing infants. Let the bridegroom leave his room, and the bride her chamber.

Again, I felt the Holy Spirit compel me to hit the pause button. I couldn't have imagined what God was about to do, but I was sure He wanted me to call our church to an extended time of fasting, prayer, and worship. So, I gathered my staff and told them what God was leading us to do. I had never done this before and had no clue what it was about. But I was certain this was from God.

When Ken was pastor, he routinely scheduled a spring and fall revival. But, we hadn't scheduled a "revival" in the three years since Ken retired. People asked me on a regular basis, "When are we going to have a revival?" My answer would always go something like, "That's a great question. I pray it begins today."

Back in the day, spring and fall revivals were a great method designed to revive believers and reach unbelievers. But, I felt scheduling a week of meetings had run its course. Besides, you can't schedule revival. Revival only happens when God's people repent. I felt people had come to depend on a scheduled event rather than a movement of the Spirit of God. So, we decided to take "revivals" off the calendar and wait.

We had already broken ground on our new auditorium and our grand opening was scheduled in September. One of my staff members suggested that God might be calling us to this "Sacred Gathering" to prepare us for the people who would flood to our new building. It sounded good and we tried to connect the dots. But, we would soon find out that our new building had nothing to do with what God was about to do. Ironically, it was the opposite. It wasn't about getting people into our building at all; it was about getting the church out of the building, into the community, and around the world.

Kyle had heard a guy named Jeff Lewis speak on prayer and fasting at a Passion One Day (www.passion oneday.com) event several years earlier. So, I decided to give him a call. Jeff was an Assistant Professor of Intercultural Studies and the Director of the Global Center at California Baptist University. He is, without a doubt, one of the sharpest missional thinkers I've ever met. He is incredibly articulate and knowledgeable. But, he doesn't live in an ivory tower. He is a practitioner as well as a thinker. He doesn't just talk missional; he lives missional.

My first impression of Jeff was a little strange, really. When I called to invite him to lead us through our Sacred Gathering, he wanted to ask me some questions before giving an answer. I forget all the questions he asked in our first conversation, but I remember he wasn't interested in being a part of just another event stuck on the calendar.

He wanted to know if we were serious about seeking the heart of God. I remember thinking how strange that was and, at the same time, how refreshing it was. Usually, people just look at a calendar to see if they have the date open. But, as I would soon discover, Jeff is anything but usual. He's unusual—a Paul or Elijah kind of unusual— the kind of unusual that God uses to knock people off center and capture their heart and minds for His glory.

I told Jeff what I felt God leading us to do and that we really had no clue why or what it was about. But, I knew God wanted to reveal His heart to our church. Jeff said something that seemed so obvious I didn't even acknowledge it at the moment. He said, "Pat, if you really want to seek the heart of God, you're going to find that His heart is for the nations."

No matter how hard we try not to, we tend to read the Bible very individualistically. Our Western cultural mindset is to read Scripture from our perspective and interpret it as if it's all about us. But, God's Word doesn't tell us specifically who to marry, where to live, what career path to follow, what job to take, or what state to live in. Neither will we find specific directions for individual churches. What we will find is God's heart and direction for His people and His church.

I learned a great spiritual principle from Henry Blackaby's book, *Experiencing God.* The principle described where LifePoint really needed to be in order to hear from God. Blackaby said,

> What is God's will for my life—is not the right question. I think the right question is, what is God's will? Once I know God's will, then I can adjust my life to Him . . . Once I know what God

is doing, then I know what I need to do. The focus needs to be on God, not *my life!*[5]

So, "What's God's will for my life?" is the wrong question because the focus really isn't God's will; it's your life. The right question is, "What's God's will?" because the focus is on God.

So, "What is God's heart for our church?" is the wrong question. The correct question is, "What is God's heart?" because the focus is not our church; the focus is God's heart. And, as Jeff said, God has clearly revealed that His heart is for the nations.

I'm sure our people thought I had eaten some funny mushrooms when I told them God wanted us to fast for three days and gather at night for prayer and worship. I know they thought I didn't have both oars in the water when I said I wasn't going to preach and that I had no clue what these meetings were about. I only knew God was up to something beyond what we could imagine, and He wanted to reveal Himself to us.

The experiences, conversations, and heartshift during what we called our "Sacred Gathering" were truly beyond what we could have imagined or planned. But, it wasn't possible without a high level of commitment from our people. We asked those who were medically able to fast and drink only liquids for three days.

I also asked our staff to do a media fast for the three-day Sacred Gathering. Can you imagine life without TV, computer, cell phones, e-mail, voice mail, or social media for three hours, let alone three days? The only approved media was worship music.

I asked our church to start their fast at midnight on Sunday and we would break our fast after our Wednesday evening gathering. To be honest, I was really skeptical of the number of people who would show up. We weren't bringing in some slick communicator or popular musician. I didn't even know what our gatherings would look like. It definitely wasn't a consumer event.

Our office is usually loud and boisterous. We work hard and we laugh hard—and we do them both together. But, that Monday was different. I told all staff to lock themselves away in their office and our assistants to disturb us only in case of emergency.

I asked my staff to begin reading the book of Acts and write down everything God impressed upon their hearts and minds. We would come together each morning at 10 a.m. and Jeff would lead us through a time of prayer.

Then, we'd go drink a smoothie together.

A Sacred Gathering

Monday night rolled around and I was blown away when I walked out of my office. The place was packed. I thought the commitment was too high to motivate large numbers of people to participate.

My first conversation with Jeff made more sense after watching God use him in our first Sacred Gathering. He later commented to LifePoint Church in 2012:

> People can stand on the stage and try their best to communicate God's truth. But, at a Sacred Gathering, you are a facilitator whose desire is not to be heard—but to lead people to the throne so they can hear from God.

Jeff organized movements of worship and a guided prayer time. Sometimes, we prayed individually and sometimes with a partner and sometimes in groups, all sandwiched between times of intense worship.

I was shocked when the crowd grew bigger each night. There was nothing sexy or trendy about this event. It was actually the opposite. It was slowing down and shutting up in order to listen. It was so countercultural and it was so refreshing.

The second night, it all began to make sense. All of a sudden, adults and families with good jobs and nice houses began to come and tell me they felt God directing them to give up everything, go to another culture, and make God famous. All of a sudden, LifePoint was set ablaze with a passion for the glory of God among the nations.

One passage that God impressed upon our brains during this time is Psalm 46:10, "Be still, and know that I am God. I will be exalted among the nations. I will be exalted in the earth!"

Many of you know the first part of that verse: "Be still and know that I am God . . ." We love it because it's about us knowing God and we want to know God. But, few even realize that the second half of the verse reveals the global implication of knowing God—and it's not about us. The implication is that "I will be exalted among the nations, I will be exalted on earth." We don't just know God for our benefit; we know God for His glory. It's not about us; it's about God.

We must state and restate this mantra over and over because the gravitational pull of our heart is to make everything about us. How else do we explain the fact that most people who claim to know Jesus never share their faith with anyone? How else do we explain the fact that so many church members have participated in more Bible studies than Billy Graham, yet they're still some of the most ornery people on the planet? What else can explain the fact that most people who claim to love Jesus give less to their church than they spend on their annual supply of Girl Scout cookies?

Henry Blackaby along with Richard Blackaby and Claude King wrote a book about revival called *Fresh Encounter*. They issued an ominous warning about hearing God's voice. They said:

> God does not make suggestions. He speaks commands. Do you want God to speak to you, your family, and your church? Then be prepared to obey Him. To hear the Creator of the universe communicate with you and then refuse to do what He says is an unmitigated offense. He is your Lord. . . . He has every right to ask you whatever He pleases.[6]

Being a disciple of Jesus isn't about information; it's about transformation. The religious leaders of Jesus' day knew more religious information than anybody in town. It's how they got promoted. But, even though they had information, they had no transformation. That's why Jesus said they were like "whitewashed tombs" (Matt. 23:27). They looked good on the outside but were rotten on the inside.

Sadly, this describes so many Christians today. They have plenty of information about Jesus, but little, if any, transformation in regard to how they live.

Atheism seems to be getting greater exposure than ever. Atheists like Richard Dawkins and Christopher Hitchens are not only key thinkers and communicators; they, in essence, have become self-professed "evangelists" for their cause.

But these new atheists do not scare me. They may get Christians all fired up, but they have little influence on the world. The people who really scare me are practical atheists. These are people who claim a strong belief in Jesus, yet He makes no practical difference in the way they live. Proof of salvation isn't found in what you claim; it's found in how you live. And how we live will either be an argument for or against Jesus Christ and His movement.

We have to get this right because there are all kinds of implications if we don't. If we believe salvation is simply about people—and not also about God's glory—then our motivation to share the gospel will revolve around keeping people out of the smoking section. That's a great motivation. Snatching people from the flames of hell gets me excited. But, our ultimate motivation for sharing the gospel should be the glory of God not the eternal destiny of man.

Missions-Minded?

Before our first Sacred Gathering, asking if we were missions-minded would have been like asking somebody from the South if they liked sweet tea. Stupid question. Of course we were missions-minded. Like every good Southern Baptist church, we gave money to the Cooperative Program (CP), which is the central giving mechanism that supports Southern Baptist Convention (SBC) initiatives worldwide including international and North American missions.

The SBC is different than most denominations in that each church is totally autonomous. No one tells me or any other pastor in the SBC what to preach or how to organize for ministry, or what style music to play. No one tells us who to hire or what to do with our money.

During our Sacred Gathering, we realized we were more missions-minded than we thought, but not in the way we thought. We were missions-minded because missions was on our mind, but that was about it. We thought about missions, but we didn't *do* missions. We became painfully aware of the fact that giving money so others can do missions is a good thing, but it's a bad thing if it becomes the only thing.

The Cooperative Program was conceived and adopted in 1925 so churches could do more globally by pooling their money. I think it was a brilliant idea that has provided the resources to preach the gospel to millions of people. Many people are in heaven today because of the cooperation of thousands of churches.

But somewhere along the line, many churches basically abdicated their responsibility to do missions to a mission sending agency. The churches responsibility was reduced to "pay, pray, and stay out of the way." Give your money and let us take care of it for you.

During our Sacred Gathering, we realized we could no longer outsource missions. We could no longer sit back and basically pay someone else to do what we were commanded to do. We could no longer pay, pray, and stay out of the way. Things were about to change.

Now, before some of you get mad and start writing nasty blogs or sending trash-talking e-mails, I'm not throwing the baby out with the bath water. I'm not saying we should do away with sending agencies. Agencies are vital to accomplishing the mission God has given the church. I'm simply saying the church should no longer be content to pay, pray, and stay out of the way. The church must own the responsibility given to us by God to *do* missions and not just *think* missions. We can no more outsource missions than we can outsource someone to do our quiet time for us.

The church should be highly involved in the selection of missionaries. The church should also be involved in determining where they go and what they do. And by all means, the local church should hold missionaries accountable for doing their jobs. If we don't, we are outsourcing our God-given responsibility.

Could it be that the church has lost market share in our world because we have forgotten what we're all about? Could it be Christians have lost a passion for the souls in Jerusalem and Judea and Samaria because we've outsourced our responsibility to go to the end of the earth?

Start Here

God wanted us to see the simple solution for our man-centered hearts. But He had to go to extraordinary means for us to really understand what He wanted. We cannot possibly honor God in LifePoint's story by just explaining what we do. If God had not intervened in the way He did, when He did, we would have been just another "successful" church.

God has the same mission for every church, but how that looks will be unique to place and time. A church of fifty people in Ohio will not approach the mission of God exactly the same as a church of three thousand in Tennessee. Both are critical for making the invisible kingdom of God visible in the world. But neither will be exactly the same.

When you think of such a transition in your church and community, it can be pretty overwhelming. The obstacles and opposition grab your attention like a Christmas Eve snow in Florida. It's easy to think—"This could never happen here." But wait—there's hope.

If you hear any part of LifePoint's story, you must hear this: Every church needs defining moments when God becomes more than a name or a cause—when He becomes a living God with a voice and a will.

Every church must operate in response to hearing the voice of God. You might say, "Isn't that what every church does?" Plenty of things move a church instead of God's voice: pride, duty, morals, and history are only a few. But these will only perpetuate dead religion. Hearing God not only tells us *what* to do, but it reminds us *why* and *how* we will do it.

God is calling His church, no matter where or what size, to display His glory. For you, as it was for LifePoint, He is not looking for another "successful" church because He gets no glory according to a man-centered scorecard.

Our first Sacred Gathering in 2004 and the corresponding awakening literally shook the core of the church and its leaders. We have had two Sacred Gatherings since, one in 2008 and one in 2012. Our people have never been the same. We met God in a new way and understood the importance of operating as a people who received a "word" from God and acted on it.

The Secret Formula

I've been told that NASA space missions are off course the majority of the time. So, Mission Control was created in 1965 to help flight crews constantly adjust to fulfill their mission. Keeping in touch with Mission Control is not only the key to success, but also critical for survival.

The local church is just as unlikely to stay on course as a NASA space mission. Drifting is common for believers and our churches. If we hope to complete our mission to change our community and world, we must see the importance of prayer without ceasing. God should be mission control for the local church.

D. L. Moody once said: "Every movement of God can be traced back to a kneeling figure."[7]

As we knelt for the first time at our Sacred Gathering in 2004, we became those kneeling figures. We were not trying to become spiritual heroes, nor did we really know what to expect as we knelt. We were utterly clueless. I only knew God wanted us to pray.

The simple takeaway from LifePoint's story is prayer. And we have discovered that talking about prayer, taking prayer requests, doing prayer studies, and even having prayer rooms is nowhere near as important as praying. Nobody disagrees with prayer being critical to the mission of God—but I wonder how many people really pray. I think the role of prayer is not near as complicated as we have made it.

Out of our desperation we often fall into the trap of looking for a formula or secret to better praying. I believe we have the secret—you can stop looking. This secret is not a formula, but it will revolutionize your praying and your mission. Here it is: "The secret of prayer is praying." Like the brilliant 1988 marketing plan from Nike, sometimes the best approach is to "Just do it."

Jesus on Simple Prayer

To Jesus, prayer was simple, dynamic, and personal. We watch Him pray in Scripture as the people around Him watched Him pray in real time. They admired His effective prayer life and asked Him to be their prayer coach.

Good Jewish boys grew up reciting prayers at different times but they knew Jesus was doing something different. I don't know about you, but it's encouraging to me to know that Jesus' disciples also struggled with prayer and asked Him for help in their prayer life.

As a result of this request, God gave us the gift of one of the most famous prayers ever recorded. You've probably heard it referred to as the Lord's Prayer. Some call it the model prayer, which is probably more appropriate since that's Jesus' intent, teaching us how to pray.

I am not sure Jesus ever intended His disciples to recite this prayer verbatim, like we did for good luck before my high school football games. The heart behind the prayer is a simple relationship with someone you love, respect, and adore.

> Pray then like this: Our Father in heaven, hallowed be your name. Your kingdom come, your will be done, on earth as it is in heaven. Give us this day our daily bread, and forgive us our debts, as we also forgive our debtors. And lead us not into temptation, but deliver us from evil. (Matt. 6:9–13)

You've probably read books and heard many sermons on this prayer, so I won't spend a lot of time here. But, I do want to zoom in on two aspects of Jesus' model prayer that I think is vital to pursuing and living in obedience to the heart of God for every individual and church.

Your Kingdom Come

Jesus was teaching His disciples, then and now, that our prayers must focus on God's kingdom, not ours. God's kingdom isn't just something we enjoy when we go to heaven; it's a present reality.

> For the kingdom of God is not a matter of eating and drinking but of righteousness and peace and joy in the Holy Spirit. (Rom. 14:17)

The kingdom of God is righteousness, peace, and joy. In other words, the kingdom of God is God's rule and reign that transforms those who surrender to Jesus. So it's a present reality now that should become evident in the lives of Christ followers.

Yet, at the same time, the kingdom of God is yet to come.

> "The King will say to those on his right, 'Come, you who are blessed by my Father, inherit the kingdom prepared for you from the foundation of the world.'" (Matt. 25:34)

So, God's kingdom is a present reality, but it's also something that is not yet, something we will inherit where everything is perfect. There will be no orphan without a mom or dad to tuck her in and tell her they love her. There will be no refugee who has to run for his life. There will be no girl sold by her family and trafficked for her body. The economy will never fail. There will be no divorce and no dying. There will be no war and no hungry people. His kingdom will be perfect.

Doesn't that sound amazing? As we pray, "Your kingdom come . . ." we are praying,

> Father, I am a citizen of Your kingdom. I want to work hard to help people see Your invisible kingdom. What can I do to make this invisible kingdom visible?

This is why praying as Jesus taught us to pray is so important. We are reminded that we can't sit back and pat each other on the back because we've changed our behavior. We must personally share the gospel, fight injustice, and serve the marginalized so that God's name will be exalted among the nations.

Your Will Be Done

We don't converse with our King to bend Him to our will and get Him to do what we want; we converse with Him in prayer so that He can bend us to His will and motivate us to do what He wants. Remember Jesus' prayer in the Garden of Gethsemane? He prayed, "Daddy, I don't want to do this—but I want Your will more than My own."

Prayer is not about getting what we want or changing God's mind; prayer is about changing us. It's about bringing me into alignment with the heart and will of God so I can know, love, and trust Him and be involved in what He is up to in the world.

My natural bent is for prayer to be about me. But my response to God should be: "More than I want what I want—I want You. I want Your will for my life, work, family, and church."

That is what made the Sacred Gatherings so important for us. We were coming together to surrender our desires, our lives, and our church to the will and heart of God. And He gladly took hold of them for His glory!

Since this awakening, LifePointers have been doing things we have never done before, all over the world. But it has not always been that way. Everything started when we paused to seek the heart of God through prayer and fasting. It was then that He shaped us to be something different so we could do something different for His glory.

✝ *LifePoints . . .*

The 2004 Sacred Gathering was the catalyst for all that has happened at LifePoint. We set aside three days for prayer, fasting, and seeking God corporately. During that time He set our faces toward the nations and we made a commitment to go to the nations for the fame of His name. **—Kyle**

~~~~~~~~~

Prepping for our first Sacred Gathering, Pat cast the vision: "We want to know God's heart." And Jeff Lewis, who God used incredibly through our gatherings, seemed to be warning us when we invited him: "Know if I come, I will share God's heart is for the nations." We didn't realize the magnitude of that statement. We were prepping for growth because of a new building; God was preparing us to leave the building. **—Jason**

~~~~~~~~~

When we had our very first Sacred Gathering, I knew that we were on the verge of something big. I saw a church participate in a three-day fast, come together and pray fervently for three nights. He brought LifePoint to its knees and we haven't looked back. It was a pivotal time in the life of our church. And the best is yet to come. **—Amy**

Moving Forward . . .

1. What steps can you take to make hearing God's voice a priority in your life?

2. How can you make hearing God's voice a priority in your public gatherings?

Chapter 6

Sacred to Us, but Useless to God

May God be gracious to us and bless us
and make his face to shine upon us,
that your way may be known on earth,
your saving power among all nations.

(PSALM 67:1–2)

WHEN WE OPENED OUR new auditorium in 2004, the multipurpose room where we worshipped was converted into a full-time gym. Our people were pumped about being able to have open gym nights and starting sports leagues at the church. But, as they say, "The best laid plans of mice and men . . ."

After our Sacred Gathering, we realized a recreation ministry was not in alignment with the direction God had revealed to us. Please don't get me wrong; many churches have used recreation facilities as a bridge to reach many people with the gospel. So, I'm not bashing rec ministry in any way.

But, after God had renewed our passion for His glory among the nations and our role in it, spending thousands of dollars to build fields and buy equipment no longer made sense. That would require our people to give more time at the building and continue to promote the idea that everything needs to happen in or around the building.

Our culture needed to change. Turning back was not an option. We were convinced that people needed to get out of the building and get more involved in the city rec leagues. We were also convinced that providing an on-campus "Christian" rec league would require our people to keep spending time with people on our turf rather than building intentional relationship with people on their turf.

Crazy Values

So, we decided to give our new basketball goals away. People thought we were crazy. We hadn't had them long and they weren't cheap. But, we knew the longer we used them, the harder it would be for our people to get rid of them. So we gave them to a local school and reminded our people of Jesus' commission to "go." Our values had shifted. Tough decisions were required to help us transition from an inwardly focused culture to an outwardly focused culture.

One of our strategies to accomplish this culture change was to train coaches to go into our community rec leagues. Their passion for sports would give them a platform to intentionally rub shoulders with people from the community.

Our city was rapidly growing with young families. As a result, there are so many kids signing up to play sports that there weren't enough coaches or practice fields to meet the demands of the growing number of teams.

So we met with our city rec department and told them we had forty-two acres of land. If they wanted to develop some of the land into ball fields, they were welcome to it. They were excited about the possibility, but didn't want to spend the money and time to develop fields that would be used for church league sports. We assured them we weren't interested in church leagues. We wanted to serve our community, not compete with it. We wanted to provide coaches for their leagues and land for their fields.

I'm not saying this shift was easy or that everyone was happy. Some were upset that they could no longer play basketball in the gym on Thursday nights, or that we wouldn't be starting recreational leagues. But God had given us a picture of His people living sent lives. We could no longer talk a good game about being missions-minded; we would prove it with our actions.

Sacred to Us, but Useless to God

In chapter 4, I talked about God's presence being in a place in the Old Testament—the Holy of Holies. In the Gospels, God's Presence was in a person—Jesus Christ. But, since the day of Pentecost in Acts, God's presence indwells all who repent and surrender to Him. Those people are His church. Here is the progression:

- God's Presence in a Building—*The Temple*
- God's Presence in a Person—*Jesus Christ*
- God's Presence in a People—*The Church*

Jesus was sent as the first cross-cultural missionary. Then, He said, "As the Father has sent me; I am sending you." So, the church is not a building, the church is people that have been redeemed by Jesus and sent by Him into our community and world to make much of Him. I know that sounds basic. You've heard it so many times; we had heard it too. But we weren't living it.

It's like that warning label on the pack of cigarettes that says, "Warning, smoking is hazardous to your health." All smokers have read this many times and they even know it to be true, but it obviously doesn't affect them if they continue to light up the burnt offerings.

We had read, and even preached, so many times that the church isn't a building; it's the people. I mentioned the Great Commission at least twice a month. We knew the Bible said, "Go!" But, rather than going to the community and world, we just kept coming to the building. We knew that Jesus said, "As the Father has sent Me, I am sending you." But, rather than living sent, we kept living safe.

So we had this truth, but it didn't really have us. It wasn't until God overwhelmed us and opened our eyes to see and our minds to understand this dynamic, explosive, and living truth, that LifePoint was radically altered. When this basic theology moved from our brains to our hearts, we could no longer play church or live safe, sheltered, or inwardly focused lives.

With this truth came a shocking, if not embarrassing, discovery about LifePoint Church. We were very "successful" in the church world. We had many butts in seats, a growing budget, and new buildings. But, God had opened our eyes and changed our scorecard. We learned our methods and mind-sets were sacred to us, but they were useless to God.

Everything must be held with an open hand if God is going to truly get glory from His people. All our ambitions, plans, and scorecards can get in the way of His true mission for the church if they are about anything but His glory.

We realized that God was not trying to make us into a better version of ourselves (much to our disappointment). A better version of me can lead to pride and the temptation to take credit. I have discovered that the best version of Pat Hood is the dead version. It's when I die to myself and live for the heart of God through the empowering of the Holy Spirit that indwells my soul.

Remember the marching orders that Jesus gave His disciples just before He went back to heaven in Acts 1:8:

> You will receive power when the Holy Spirit has come upon you, and you will be my witnesses in Jerusalem and in all Judea and Samaria, and to the end of the earth.

Matthew recorded it this way:

> Go therefore and make disciples of all nations, baptizing them in the name of the Father and of the Son and of the Holy Spirit, teaching them to observe all that I have commanded you. And behold, I am with you always, to the end of the age. (Matt. 28:19–20)

Jesus commissioned every believer to be a missionary. The "what" has been determined for everyone who follows Him. The "how" and the "where" are the only questions. And the "how" and the "where" may change numerous times over the course of your life.

I am amazed by the fact that LifePointers, for the most part, have refused to ask God for the details before saying "yes" to His direction for their lives. Instead, they have been crazy sensitive to God's momentary assignment. And just like Elisha (see chapter 3), they scrapped everything they were currently focused on in order to obey immediately.

Plenty of examples of instantaneous obedience can be found in the Bible. The most famous examples were the disciples:

And he said to them, "Follow me, and I will make you fishers of men." Immediately they left their nets and followed him. (Matt. 4:19–20)

Jesus invited His disciples to leave everything and follow Him. Today, they would've probably spent weeks or months in "prayer." I put quotes around prayer because it's a common hiding place for the believer. Rather than immediate obedience, it's so easy to hide behind prayer. But that's not what the disciples did. They couldn't obey fast enough. When God speaks, you shouldn't have to pray about obeying.

The Instantly Obedient Heart

God created something new at LifePoint that I can't explain. In fact, if I tried to explain what He has done, I'm afraid my humanity would take over and I would be tempted to take credit in some way. I would try to appear brilliant—this is how we scripted this incredible LifePoint transition from struggle to success, from success to significance, and from significance to sending.

The bottom line is, God revealed Himself and created an environment where people were just crazy enough to respond in immediate obedience. No matter how well you preach, you can never make that happen. Only God can change the hearts and minds of people.

You might ask, "Well, did a construction executive making six figures not even stop for a minute and count the cost of obedience?" I don't want to over-spiritualize here, so let me say *of course* those thoughts ran through the minds of numerous LifePointers who left all. But, they didn't count the cost for long, because they would have said "no" if they did.

I can't give you steps to create that environment. But once people began to crave knowing God, then immediate obedience became the only logical next step. Let me unpack that for you by looking again at Psalm 46:10: "Be still, and know that I am God. I will be exalted among the nations, I will be exalted in the earth!"

1. Be Still. Psalm 46 was a song given by God to a people who were terrified of their enemies. Battles and wars were a way of life for people in that time in history. The only thing that was certain was uncertainty. Life was one big game of king of the mountain—literally.

Did you ever play king of the mountain as a kid? One kid stood on a hill and we attacked him from every angle trying to take his spot. The only rule was—there were no rules! Any way you can knock him off the hill was legal. Some of us still play that game in our jobs and churches—sad to say. And this makes life very stressful and anxious.

The word from God through the psalmist in Psalm 46 was "be still" or "just stop!" "Stop all the worrying about the next bad thing that might happen. Stop being so restless and frantically looking for your next big break. Take the focus off yourself and put it on Me."

2. Know that I Am God. Although we looked very "successful," I believe we were headed down a path of restless, consumer Christianity. We were so satisfied with something good, that we almost missed the greatest thing God has put His people on earth to do—live sent lives for the fame of His name. Little did we know that we were about to miss the heartbeat of God and reject an invitation to "know Him" in ways beyond our imaginations.

People live their entire lives trying to replace bad behaviors with good ones. We call that "behavior modification." In the church world, we call it religion and it has nothing to do with knowing God or experiencing His power. And the way many churches attempt to preach, teach, and disciple amounts to little more than how to modify people's behavior.

Knowing God goes far beyond being good people. Knowing God means more than knowing facts about Him; it means having a dynamic, personal, life-giving relationship with the Creator of all things. It's the difference between knowing who Bono is and knowing my wife.

I know lots of facts about Bono, but I don't know him. I know Bono was born as Paul David Hewson in 1960. He fronts one of the most successful rock bands in history—U2. I know the band began in Dublin, Ireland, in 1978.

I know that Bono is quite an activist and a cool-looking dude. But I don't really *know* him. We have never hung out or had a conversation. If he passed me in a crowd, he wouldn't recognize me or know my name. I know a lot about him and could learn more if I wanted—through the miracle that is Google. But I do not know him and he does not know me.

Now, my wife, Amy, is a totally different subject. I also know a lot of facts about her. Her name is Amy Rebecca Hood. Her maiden name is Nunley. She's from a large family, two sisters and a brother. Amy was a surprise to her parents. Her mom was forty-two when she was born. So, she was as spoiled as month-old milk, which makes life hard for me.

I could go on and on. But, I know more than facts; I really know her. I know what makes her happy. She adores our kids and she loves to travel. I also know what makes her sad—orphans. She is a tireless advocate for the fatherless as a volunteer Orphan Director for a nonprofit called OneLess (onelessministries.org). She loves to ride on the back of my Harley. Her heart leaps at the thought of traveling internationally.

Can you see the difference between knowing about Bono and knowing Amy? Amy does not have an article about her in Wikipedia and has never performed in sold-out arenas around the world. But she is a rock star in my world! We have an amazing relationship and I trust her completely because I know her heart.

Knowing God in the original Hebrew language means to be intimate with Him and to know His heart. To know God is to know what He loves, what He hates, what makes Him happy, and what makes Him angry. Once you really know God on that level, you have distaste for anything less. Even religion becomes repulsive apart from knowing God personally.

3. I Will Be Exalted. Jesus' death isn't just about knowing God; it's much deeper. There's a global implication to knowing God. He didn't just save us *from* something; He saved us *for* something. He saved us to live for the fame of His name so that He'll receive the global worship, praise, and honor that He deserves.

John 3:16 is arguably the most famous verse in the Bible. Tim Tebow brought it to the world's attention when he wrote it on his eye black while winning the Heisman trophy at the University of Florida. We see it tagged in spray paint on underpasses and old buildings in cities all over America. If you know the verse, you love the verse. But, unfortunately, we have been guilty of making the verse all about us!

> For God so loved the world, that he gave his only Son, that whoever believes in him should not perish but have eternal life. (John 3:16)

John 3:16 is a great verse, but it's not about me—it's about God giving His Son for the world. So, it's not just personal, it's global. I am saved by God for the glory of God. I am saved for 7,051,803,904 people (men, women, and children) at the moment of this writing.[8]

The first Christians got it. They knew saying "yes" to Jesus changed everything. Their job was no longer just a job; it was their mission. Raising their kids wasn't about getting them out of the house; it was about raising warriors who fought for the glory of God. It meant that every domain of their life was a context to make Him famous.

But they also realized it was bigger than their little world. They realized that God had called them to be global Christians by representing Him to all nations. And they were to promote Him everywhere.

That's why Psalm 46:10 has become one of my favorite verses in the Bible. It's not just about me knowing God personally, it's also about the implication of knowing Him—that He would be known and exalted among the nations.

Giving Ourselves Away

The Sacred Gathering changed everything. We realized that we had given money to missions, but we hadn't given ourselves. We prayed, but we didn't go. This had to change.

Jesus said, "Go." Giving money is important, but giving money to help others go doesn't absolve me of my mandate to go. I shouldn't give money instead of going; I should give money and go . . . to my office, to the ball field, to school, to my house, and around the world. So we knew we had to get busy. We had to get our hands dirty and invest our lives, not just our money.

Remember Acts 1:8? Jesus told His followers, "You will be my witnesses in Jerusalem and in all Judea and Samaria, and to the end of the earth." Jesus wasn't saying we should go to those places in concentric order. His commission was to go to those closest to us *and* to those on the other side of the world simultaneously.

Believers shouldn't have to wait for the church to organize a mission project for them to live missionally. They should go locally as an organic outflow of their regenerate heart. But going across the pond requires some strategic organization and planning.

So, we planned some intentional mission experiences in order to help our people obey Jesus' command to go to the ends of the earth. But the last thing we wanted to do was "one-off" mission "trips."

"One-offs" are what we call trips where people go to a location once, but usually don't return. The mission of "one-offs" is as much about the experience of the people going as it is about the people they are serving.

Don't get me wrong; we want our people to have an incredible experience. But our people's experience is not primary. The primary purpose is to meet the specific needs of a people group in order to establish a context for sharing the gospel and planting churches.

So our strategy was to develop partnerships with ministries or missionaries who served specific people groups. We didn't want to send a team, come home, present a slide show, and move on to the next event. We wanted to develop a presence where we could invest in a people group for the long haul. We wanted to send teams, money, resources, and build long-term relationships with a specific people group so we could earn their trust and help them know the love and grace of God.

First Steps—the Favelas

We established our first partnership in South America. One of the members of LifePoint had a connection with a missionary near a large South American city whose name was, we'll say, Joe Brown.

We took a vision trip to meet Joe and see his ministry, which focuses on several favelas, communities of small shacks, around the city. The people in the favelas live in some of the worst poverty imaginable. The streets are covered in raw sewage. Their homes are shanty houses built by cardboard, plywood, tin, or whatever material they can find to keep off the rain and wind.

The women prostituted themselves to have enough cash to buy rice for their kids. If you saw images of people living in the New Orleans Superdome after Hurricane Katrina in 2005, then you can get an idea of what people's lives in the favelas are like. About fifty thousand people live in an area the size of a football arena in most big cities.

The police and other emergency personnel do not go in the favelas. If someone is in need of emergency care, they're out of luck. If they are lucky, someone will carry them outside the favela and lay them on the street to be picked up by the ambulance.

Justice is handled internally. Not long before we arrived, Joe told us about a man who abused a little boy in the favela. He hasn't abused anyone since. As a matter of fact, he hasn't been seen since.

The favelas are controlled by drug lords. So, outsiders do not enter unless they have the protection of the drug lord. In order to minister to this neglected people group, Joe did something that would make many church culture people cringe, he developed a relationship with the drug lord, who finally trusted him enough to give him permission to start a ministry center in the midst of the favelas.

The first time I went in, I was more nervous than a teenager on his first date. To make matters worse, Amy was with me. I wasn't worried about me. I was worried about what might happen to her if things went south. But, we were assured that we were going in under the protection of the drug lord. If anybody even spoke negatively to us, it would be the last words they spoke.

It was exciting and unnerving at the same time. I was thinking, *Do I really want to bring our people to this place? It's dangerous.* But, the task of going isn't for those who want to live safe lives. It's for those who are willing to take huge risks for the fame of God. It's not for the faint of heart. It's for those bold enough to risk everything for the sake of the gospel.

I remember seeing the kids running through the raw sewage in the streets wearing nothing but their under-wear. It was all they knew. It was a typical day in their world. I soon realized that the hopelessness in the eyes of the people was greater than the fear in my heart.

To be honest, I didn't have a passion to go to this part of the world. My passion is to go to unreached or unen-gaged people groups. We wanted to go where there aren't enough Christians in a people group to have a viable min-istry of reproduction.

This part of South America is a harvest area with many believers and many missionaries. Why send more money and more resources when there are people groups that have no Christians or missionaries at all? Then, it became obvious that this people group was a neglected people group and my perspective totally changed.

Joe had been given a building in the center of the favela to use as a ministry center. When he arrived, he was like the pied piper walking through town. Hundreds of kids came running from everywhere to get a piece of candy or a new pair of flip-flops.

The goal of our ministry is centered on sharing the gospel and then leading the adults through chronological Bible studies. But our focus is holistic ministry. So we also teach the women skills so they can make crafts and other items that can be sold in the USA so they don't have to sell their bodies to survive.

Our purpose for going to places like this South American town was to start a church planting movement that would multiply disciples, leaders, and churches. Our objective isn't to hand out clothes or give shoes to barefoot people. Nor, is it to give food to hungry people.

Meeting social needs is very important. When you see kids emaciated from starvation, you can't just walk away and go eat your steak. When you see people walk through raw sewage with bare feet, it's hard to go home and make the hard decision of which pair of shoes to wear today.

Jesus cared about the needs of people. He met needs by healing disease and feeding thousands of hungry people. But, Jesus' mission wasn't social ministry, as important as it is. His mission was redeeming lost souls.

People followed him from town to town and listened to His teaching because He met their needs. He gave them bread to fill their stomach so that He could teach them that He was the Bread of Life. He healed their physical diseases to teach them that He was the Great Physician who could heal their spiritual disease.

Our mission wasn't social; it was spiritual. We simply met social needs to open the door to teach the spiritual truth. The last thing we want to do is meet someone's temporal need and watch them go to hell for all eternity. Our mission is the gospel.

Each year, we send several teams to this South American city. We've gone back so many times that some of our people have relationships with some of the people in the favelas. They know our people by name and our people know their names.

We've seen many people redeemed. We've planted a church in one favela that is ministering to the needs of its own. We've built another church building and trained many leaders. Slowly, but surely, we're seeing a movement begin to take place.

Next Steps: Bihar

Tim Patterson served as a missionary with the International Mission Board (IMB) of the SBC in Central and South America for eighteen years, but he was in the process of making a transition to Bihar, India. He would be in the States about a year before he moved to India. So, he and his wife decided to move to Smyrna and attended LifePoint, where his sister is a member.

When the Pattersons finally left for India, we made a commitment that he wouldn't go alone. We were now his Sending Church and they would not be forgotten. Our plan was to develop a partnership with Bihar after he arrived.

After the Pattersons landed in Bihar, I took a small group of leaders to explore the partnership. We were stunned when we discovered that this region of India had larger unreached and unengaged people groups than any other part of the world. There are two hundred people groups in Bihar and eighty of them are completely untouched with the gospel.

One of these people groups is the Yadav people. There are approximately eleven million Yadav in Bihar, living in thirty-nine thousand villages, without any presence of the story of Jesus. They give their devotion and worship to false gods, and we wanted to change that. So, we rented a facility to house and train men and women who had been transformed by Jesus.

In this part of the world, when you're found by Jesus, you generally lose your family. Sometimes, a dad might kill his son or a husband might kill his wife if she declared

Jesus as Savior. At best, you would be disowned and thrown out.

Sometimes, the family has a funeral to make a statement that their child is dead to them. So, Jesus' words, "If anyone would come after me, let him deny himself and take up his cross daily" (Luke 9:23) really mean something in this part of the world. Giving your life to Jesus meant giving up everything.

Our facility in Bihar provided a place to disciple new believers and train them to start indigenous churches. We began sending LifePoint teams to facilitate training, ministry, and evangelism.

Just a few steps—living sent at home

When Jesus told His first disciples to go, He wasn't just talking about packing up and moving to some other country to be cross-cultural missionaries, although some would. Every moment of every day as they walked through their village, shopped at the local market, and went to dinner at a friend's house they were on mission. Every domain of their lives was a mission field.

Membership at LifePoint became about joining God in His global mission (versus taking advantage of the goods and services of a local church). Doing your part to spread the fame of His name to every people group is owned by every member of LifePoint. We no longer wanted more members for our church. We wanted more missionaries for God's kingdom.

Paul was addressing a highly religious and deeply intellectual crowd in Athens, Greece, when God gave him some great truth. He said that God "made from one man every nation of mankind to live on all the face of the earth, having determined allotted periods and the boundaries of their dwelling place" (Acts 17:26).

You know what that means for you? God created you in this specific time in history and placed you exactly where you are to be a missionary. You live in the exact house, in the exact neighborhood, in the exact city, by God's plan and for His glory. You are there to be a missionary for a specific time.

How do you think the dreams and ambitions of Christians would change if they really got this amazing truth? What impact do you think it would have on our world? If you realized that your job was not a means for you to make enough money to pay the bills or buy toys, but it was actually your mission field, how would it change your view of work? Your job is your platform to make relationships and make disciples. You don't just get up every day to go do what you do; you're a missionary to the nations.

In Scripture, the word *nations* doesn't mean geopolitical countries. Nations describes a group of people bound together by a specific culture and language. The Yadav people in India are a people group bound together by a specific language and culture. But, so are athletes, artists, businessmen, and rednecks. These are all people groups bound together by a specific culture and language.

People who wear Wrangler jeans and have a deer head hanging on their wall are a nation of people. They think differently than a nation of people who drive sports cars and wear Versace. And God has called all types of believers to go into their domain and spread the fame of His name among these people groups.

So, if you're a Christ follower, the question is not "Are you called to missions?" The call to Christ is a call to missions. The question is, "What is the application?" Some of you may apply your calling by moving to a different country. But most of you will apply your calling by coaching football or practicing law or repairing engines. You take your personality, passion, skills, and experience and apply them in every domain of your life to make worshippers of all people.

One of the largest employers in Smyrna is Nissan. LifePoint is privileged to be home to many Nissan employees. We constantly remind our Nissan people that they're not at Nissan to make cars; God has placed them at Nissan to make disciples. Nissan doesn't know it, but they're paying the salary of Christians to be missionaries. How cool is that?

We have vocational missionaries in many countries all over the world. But we have thousands of missionaries in companies, schools, businesses, and homes all over Middle Tennessee. God is just as pleased with the missionary auto mechanic at Nashville Motor Cars as He is with someone who moves to Bangkok to preach the gospel and serve orphans. Where has God assigned you to be a missionary?

⚡ LifePoints . . .

Nine years ago I came to LifePoint a selfish, consumer-minded church-goer. Today my family and I have been on a three-year path to follow God's will for us to become global missionaries. We have been encouraged, challenged, and strengthened by this church family. I am a person seeking God's will and not my own. **—Cynthi**

Through the influence of friends at LifePoint, my family went on our first mission trip. We saw firsthand how God works through LifePoint to change lives. Our experiences on that trip have led us to take several other mission trips and have given me a heart for serving through missions and supporting missionaries. **—Tony**

~~~~~~~~

My first out-of-the-country mission trip with LifePoint was to Sao Paulo, Brazil. There, God showed me that loving Him was loving people and being intentional about sharing the gospel with them. I saw that people who are in extreme poverty and in difficult situations long for someone to just love them and show that they care. Love is a universal language that transcends culture and can break down any barriers to share the gospel. **—Cortney**

Moving Forward . . .

1. What do you need to let go in order to be more missional?

2. What can you or your church give away to meet a need for God's glory?

3. Are any methods at your church sacred to you, but useless to God?

Chapter 7

A Costly "Ask"

Whoever does not bear his own cross and come after me cannot be my disciple. . . . So therefore, any one of you who does not renounce all that he has cannot be my disciple.

(LUKE 14:27, 33)

REAL OBEDIENCE IS ALWAYS costly. When I surrendered my life to Christ, it cost me the right to dream my own dreams and plan my own future. When I moved to seminary, it cost me proximity to my family and lifelong friends, along with the comfort of a familiar world. The many changes that have been made over the last eighteen years at FBC Smyrna/LifePoint, have cost me the color of my hair, many nights' sleep, and some good friends who didn't want to make the changes necessary to go where God was leading.

LifePoint's obedience to passionately pursue God's heart for the nations by becoming a Sending Church has cost us many incredible leaders like Kyle Goen, my Executive Pastor, Brittany Kahmin, my Director of Preschool Ministries, and some of the best marketplace leaders in our church.

Obedience to God's direction also cost us our Lead Student Pastor, David McCaman, when he and his wife, Jennifer, moved their family to Bangkok, Thailand, to become our Bangkok Campus Pastor.

I knew from the day we hired David that he would one day serve as a pastor. With each passing year, I saw this desire grow in David, along with his preaching skills. I knew he was getting restless as he waited for his opportunity to move to this next step of leadership.

In July 2010, David was leading our students at our annual student camp. Even though it was a huge week for David, I gave him a call and asked him if he would pray about becoming our Bangkok Campus Pastor.

A distraction is the last thing a student pastor needs during camp week. It's game time. It'd be like pecking a head football coach on the shoulder during the conference championship game and asking him if he was interested in another job. I knew it could distract David, but I called him anyway.

I didn't know it at the time, but David told me later that he and Jennifer had already been praying and had decided to talk with me after camp about the next step in his ministry. Obviously, we were beginning to see God's sovereign plan unfold. So, after spending a few weeks in prayer and discussion, David and Jennifer felt it was God's plan for them to move to Bangkok.

David and Jennifer's obedience to God's leadership cost them proximity to their family and friends as they moved to the other side of the world. Their obedience cost them cash as they gave up their salary and were forced to raise money. It cost them comfort as they moved into a new culture and would be forced to learn a new language.

But, it wasn't just costly for David and Jennifer; it was also costly for their parents who would lose proximity to them and, more importantly, their new grandson. It was costly to LifePoint as we lost an incredible student pastor, a tremendous leader, and an excellent communicator.

The task is difficult and the stakes are high. So, we must be willing to send our greatest resource—our people—to accomplish the mission God has given the church. Every leader we send to another country has been a strong, high-level leader at our local campuses.

Think about it—would it be smart to send weak leaders to accomplish such a great task?

I must confess, I've never been happy about this. A part of me really doesn't want to send our highest-level leaders to lead somewhere else. I want them leading by my side. They're great leaders in the marketplace and they're usually some of our top givers. They're the movers and shakers, the go-to men and women that know how to get things done.

Good stewardship isn't just about money. Time and time again, I've found that the stewardship principle always holds true in every area of life; to get, you've got to give. When you work out, you give away all your energy and leave yourself depleted. But, a funny thing happens an hour later, you have more energy than ever.

The same thing is true with leadership. If you hoard it, other leaders won't rise up. But, if you give them away, God will replace them many times over. So, don't be afraid to send your best and brightest leaders. You shouldn't send anything less if you want to be effective.

The Cost of Obedience

Obedience always comes at a high price. That's why Jesus said,

If anyone comes to me and does not hate his own father and mother and wife and children and brothers and sisters, yes, and even his own life, he cannot be my disciple. (Luke 14:26)

If anyone would come after me, let him deny himself and take up his cross daily and follow me. (Luke 9:23)

Obedience costs us everything, even our lives. This kind of obedience is sometimes hard for me to wrap my brain around. It's easier to grasp obedience when it involves supporting a child in another country for $30 per month. Or, when we take a name from the Angel Tree and spend a few dollars to make Christmas special for a needy child. It's not difficult to think about obedience in these realms because they don't really cost us that much. But, at some point, people need to understand that true obedience costs more than some pocket change and a little time.

Many look at people who obey God on a high level as weird, abnormal, or fanatical because they willingly give up some really cool stuff and don't seem to care. But, the secret is, they do care.

When they move their teenagers from the safety and security of a great local high school, they care. When sick and aging grandparents are left thousands of miles behind, they care. When some of the "creature comforts" of home are sold or left behind, they care. When they risk losing their job or their friends for sharing their faith, they care.

Jesus dramatically illustrated the cost of obedience when He gave the crowd those mind-boggling words in Luke 14 . . . the ones about hating your father, mother, wife, children, etc. And normally this is the time when the preacher steps in and bails you out saying, "That is not what Jesus was really saying." But I am not going to bail you out. I want you to pause and feel the weight of what real obedience looked like to Jesus.

Now granted, there was an original context (time, place, people) where Jesus spoke these words. When He said *hate*, He was saying we should "love less." Jesus often used hyperbole to make a point. But, that doesn't detract from the weight of Jesus' words or give us an escape clause. Bottom line, we must be willing to sacrifice everything for His mission.

Jesus talked a lot about feasts, banquets, and celebrations in Luke 14. These elements were huge in the celebratory culture of Judaism. People approached life with great passion and loved any occasion to do it up big.

Jesus illustrated the invitation of eating "bread in the kingdom of God" as being invited to a great banquet.

When one of those who reclined at table with him heard these things, he said to him, "Blessed is everyone who will eat bread in the kingdom of God!" But he said to him, "A man once gave a great banquet and invited many. And at the time for the banquet he sent his servant to say to those who had been invited, 'Come, for everything is now ready.' But they all alike began to make excuses. The first said to him, 'I have bought a field, and I must go out and see it. Please have me excused.' And another said, 'I have bought five yoke of oxen, and I go to examine them. Please have me excused.' And another said, 'I have married a wife, and therefore I cannot come.' So the servant came and reported these things to his master. Then the master of the house became angry and said to his servant, 'Go out quickly to the streets and lanes of the city, and bring in the poor and crippled and blind and lame.' And the servant said, 'Sir, what you commanded has been done, and still there is room.' And the master said to the servant, 'Go out to the highways and hedges and compel people to come in, that my house may be filled. For I tell you, none of those men who were invited shall taste my banquet.'" (Luke 14:15–24)

But, the people that were invited had better things to celebrate. And in reality, no excuse given in the RSVPs would have been considered evil—materialistic and temporary maybe—but not evil:

- New property (v. 18)
- New livestock (v. 19)
- A new wife (v. 20)

All of these things provide perfectly good occasions to celebrate. All of them are the kind of things "normal" people chase. No crime, no corruption, no Ponzi schemes—normal pursuits considered by Christ followers as blessings from God—but that was not the point. These perfectly honest pursuits become evil when they take Jesus' place in our life or become "excuses" not to do what God wants us to do.

The original word in the Greek means, "to beg a person's release." In essence, "My honor binds me to consider your invitation, I cannot ignore it, but I have more important things to celebrate."

The crowds were growing, but they had no idea Jesus was headed toward Jerusalem to die. When Jesus invites us on a journey with Him, He is inviting us to die.

Jesus wanted them, and us, to count the cost of following Him. So, He equated following Him to taking up a cross. This would have been a little hard for Jesus' crowd to wrap their brains around.

The cross had nothing to do with Christianity at the time. As a matter of fact, there was no such thing as Christianity at the time because Jesus had not yet died on the cross. So, what was He talking about?

They knew what a cross was. They had watched people die on the cross. They had seen people hang in agony on the cross for days. They knew the cross meant death. So, there was nothing beautiful, sentimental, or sacred about it at the time. It was hated and loathed because it was a symbol of oppression and execution. It would be like Jesus telling a crowd in 2013 that, in order to follow Him, they had to take a lethal injection.

Think about it—when Jesus' listeners saw someone carrying a cross in their day, whether it be friend, foe, or family, that was the last time they ever saw them! Carrying a cross meant you were going to die. What a profound picture of obeying Jesus.

But keep in mind that, although the message scared many people away, the people that kept following Jesus knew what they were signing up for. So, were they weird, fanatical, or abnormal? No, they were obedient! They fully understood and embraced Jesus' "ask."

We Lose but We Win

But, there's another side of the obedience coin. Obedience is costly, but the cost doesn't begin to compare to the rewards it guarantees. Surrendering my life to Christ cost me the right to make my own decisions and dream my own dreams. But it opened the door to living the great adventure of God's plan and future. Moving to seminary cost me proximity to family and friends. But the rewards of getting to know and serve the great people of LifePoint Church have been mind-blowing.

Making the changes we've made at LifePoint has cost me a lot of sleep and many good friends. But the rewards of seeing Jesus change the eternal destinies of people and save hundreds of marriages makes it more than worth it. The joy of seeing people begin to live on mission in the marketplace, school, and neighborhood and celebrating as people sell out and move to the other side of the world for the sake of the gospel is well worth the cost. Obedience is costly, but the rewards are far greater than any cost you could ever pay. Yes, obedience is costly, but the cost of disobedience will make you bankrupt.

Some people see Jesus as a meek and mild pacifist. But watch Him at work:

> And they came to Jerusalem. And he entered the temple and began to drive out those who sold and those who bought in the temple, and he overturned the tables of the money-changers and the seats of those who sold pigeons. And he would not allow anyone to carry anything through the temple. And he was teaching them and saying to them, "Is it not written, 'My house shall be called a house of prayer for all the nations'? But you have made it a den of robbers." (Mark 11:15–17)

Jesus was on His way to the cross. He entered the temple, started turning over tables, and running people out of town. I love this passage because it shows how strong and determined Jesus was when He walked on this planet. He wasn't some pale, wimpy male. He was masculine. He was a warrior literally fighting for the glory of God.

In Jesus' day, people worshipped in courts surrounding the temple. The outer court was the court of the Gentiles. The next court was for Jewish women. Then the men and then the priests. As you kept progressing, you finally got to the Holy of Holies in the center, which housed the ark of the covenant that symbolized God's presence among the people.

Jesus walked into the outer court and flew into a holy rage because He was surrounded by a mass of people who had lost their hunger for God and were taking advantage of people who wanted to worship God. Jesus was outraged because they showed such little passion for the nations.

Jesus also quotes Isaiah 56:6–7 when He said, "My house shall be called a house of prayer for all peoples." Now, obviously, we should pray in church, but this passage isn't saying that the church building should be a place of prayer.

Isaiah 56 is a prophecy about God bringing people from every people group into His kingdom, not just Jews. He quoted this because they had crowded out the Gentiles by setting up their tables in the court of Gentiles. They cared more for their own self-interests than the salvation of the nations. They basically said, "We're going to make some money, let the nations go to hell." They had drifted and lost focus.

Biblical anthropologists have identified thousands of unreached people groups in the world. Is it possible that we're so concerned with our own personal interests that we are basically telling the nations to go to hell? Is it possible, that we have all the resources we need to take the gospel to every people group but we have lost focus and fumbled the ball?

The Reward of the "Ask"

That's why we called LifePoint to a time of prayer and fasting; because it's so easy to become distracted from our mission and focus on our desires. We wanted to fast to say, "More than we hunger for food, we hunger for God to be 'exalted on the earth.'"

Our first Sacred Gathering was in 2004. Then, in 2008, we felt God leading us to enter another time of Sacred Gathering. We followed the same pattern as four years earlier and God again rocked our world.

Again, we felt God calling us to a deeper commitment to His glory among the nations. We had developed partnerships after our first Sacred Gathering but, this time, we began to feel God leading us to send teams to live in an unreached or unengaged people group to share the gospel and train local leaders to start indigenous churches.

On the last day of the Sacred Gathering, Kyle came to my office and said he couldn't get Belgium off his mind. I think we both knew what was happening. After weeks of discussion and prayer, I told him that if God was directing him to Belgium, then He was directing us to Belgium. I believe when God gives direction to pastors and church leaders, it's not just for their benefit; it's for the church.

I knew I had to cast this vision very clearly. I wasn't certain about how we were going to accomplish the mission, but I needed to be clear about what we were going to do.

I knew this was a big "ask." Sending people to live in another culture to share the gospel was not new to LifePoint. We had already moved a family to India to serve as vocational missionaries through the International Service Corp of the International Missions Board. We had sent a family to West Africa to serve in the same program. We had many more that felt God directing them to go somewhere; they just didn't know when or where. But this was different.

God was directing us to be the sending agency and that meant the missionaries would be our responsibility. We would select the missionaries and decide where they went. We would help develop and oversee their strategy. No longer would we simply pray for them on their birthday and send them care packages. Now, we would pray for them daily and send them whatever they needed to get the job done. They would be responsible for raising their own salary. We would pay their benefits and cover their ministry budget. This was no easy task, but nothing worthwhile ever is.

One Sunday, I was sharing the vision of sending teams of missionaries to live in Bangkok, Thailand, and Brussels, Belgium. I challenged the church to consider if God had ordained them to quit their jobs and move to Bangkok or Brussels to share the gospel and plant churches. I was more nervous about this "ask" than any I'd ever thrown on the table.

I wasn't asking people to give more money or commit to fast for three days. I was asking people to quit their jobs, sell their houses, and move their families to another country. I was asking them to learn a new language and live in another culture. I was asking them to place their kids in new schools. What if no one stepped up?

But this didn't just affect those willing to sell out and go; it affected the church as well. We would send good people away and be forced to reallocate our budget to pay for this vision. We would ask every member to either go or support those who go. It was a big "ask" and I was nervous.

Again, I was blown away when, over the next couple of months, about forty families called to say they were willing to sell out and move to Bangkok or Brussels for the glory of God. God was doing something bigger than even I could begin to grasp.

We didn't send all the families that signed up. We established a selection process that included meeting with our leadership team, marital counseling, financial counseling, and many other assessments. We told some no, some yes, and some not yet. But nothing stokes a pastor's fire like seeing so many families who are willing to obey, no matter the cost.

LifePoint Brussels and LifePoint Bangkok

Kyle and I planned a vision trip to Brussels. We made contact with the local IMB missionaries, and asked them to meet us, give us the grand tour, and brief us on the country. We spent a week exploring what God was doing in Brussels and what our role should be.

We learned that Belgium is one of the most strategic nations in Western Europe. It's also one of the most cosmopolitan nations with immigrants from all over the world. It is home for influential institutions such as the European Union and NATO. As a result, it's literally a crossroads for the world. So, we believe that if the gospel takes root there, it will spread to many nations.

Again, we had no clue why, but we also felt God leading us to send a team to Bangkok, Thailand. As we began to explore this great city, we found that Bangkok has an estimated 15 to 18 million people. Approximately one million of these 15 to 18 million are college students from all over Southeast Asia and less than 1 percent of them know Jesus as Savior.

Bangkok is like the Jerusalem of Asia in that people come there from all over the world because it offers a great education at a great price and a really low cost of living. So, much like Brussels, we believe that if the gospel can take root here, it can infect an entire continent.

The dominant religion in Thailand is Buddhism. Every time I go to Bangkok, I stay in hotels with spirit houses out front that serve as shrines to one of their many gods. But, I've noticed that Buddhists in Thailand view their religion in much the same way that many Christians in America view their faith.

Like most American cultural Christians, we found that most college students' grandparents are practicing Buddhists. Their parents were nominal Buddhists and they are cultural Buddhists, which means they are Buddhist in name only. Actually, most college students have told our missionaries that they know less about Buddhism than our missionaries.

The same is true in Brussels. Belgium is a staunch Catholic country. So, the overwhelming majority of Belgians claim to be Christian because they were baptized as a baby into Catholicism. But, when we began conversations with Belgian college students, we found that they really didn't want anything to do with Catholicism. They thought it was boring and irrelevant. Their grandparents are dedicated Catholics. Their parents are nominal Catholics and they are cultural Catholics.

The same thing is true in American Christianity. Twenty years ago, a large portion of American teenagers claimed to be Christian. Actually, 65 percent of the American World War II generation claimed to be Christian, 35 percent of the baby boomer generation claimed to be Christian and, today, only 4 percent of American teenagers claim to be Christian. America has definitely moved into a post-Christian society.[9]

LifePoint is blessed to have a strong and vibrant youth ministry with around five hundred students in our Wednesday night worship environment. Obviously, we have students at every level; many are far from God, many are strong in their faith, and many at all points in between.

We've found, experientially, that students who run hard after the heart of God come from one of two different backgrounds. They either come from homes where Mom and Dad run hard after Jesus or from homes where Mom and Dad want nothing to do with Jesus.

If a student comes from a home where Mom and Dad have a nominal faith, they usually don't want anything to do with church or Jesus. They've seen their parents claim faith but it hasn't changed their life in any way, so why should they take Jesus seriously.

Our objective in Thailand and Belgium is to start LifePoint Campuses that will reach college students and young professionals. We will disciple them to be disciple makers. Our next priority is to identify leaders and potential church planters that we will train to start local Thai-speaking churches in Thailand and French-speaking churches in Belgium.

It's important that you get this because, when I talk about starting LifePoint Campuses in other countries, most people automatically think we're starting international churches. So please read this next part really slow: our intention is not to plant international churches.

I think international churches in large urban centers around the world are an incredible strategy. There are many expats (a temporary resident from another country) living in large cities all over the world. I think it's a great strategy to reach these expats with the gospel and then send them home to take the gospel to their country. It's an incredible strategy; it just isn't what God has directed us to do.

We feel God has called us to Brussels and Bangkok (and other countries yet to be determined) to start a movement that multiplies disciples, leaders, and churches.

Our strategy is to start a campus that will allow the people we reach become a part of a healthy body so they have a picture of what they're trying to start as we send them out to start indigenous language churches.

There is no better training ground for a church planter than being involved in a healthy church. We believe there is nothing more captivating than a local body of believers living out true and authentic faith. I believe people are drawn to authentic community like a hungry dog to a raw piece of meat.

We have other campuses in the United States and our goal is for these campuses to become self-sufficient. But that's not our objective for our international campuses. Our objective is for them to reach indigenous people with the gospel, disciple them, and identify leaders we can train to be church planters. Then we will send them out with a team to plant indigenous language churches in their part of the world. We don't anticipate nor desire for them to become large churches. We hope to bring people in, train them up, and send them out.

More Than a Name Change

As a result of our vision to start campuses all over the world, we felt the need to change our name to reflect a more "global" identity. Do you know how crazy it sounds for a pastor to even mention changing the name of a 110-year-old church?

Before this, we went by the name of First Baptist Church, Smyrna. Many people had asked me to consider changing our name because they felt we were totally misrepresenting who we are. Many of their friends wouldn't come because we were First Baptist Church. They envisioned traditional music with a large choir and everybody wearing suits and acting like they have it all together. At that time, when you told someone you went to First Baptist Church, you always followed it up with "But . . . it ain't your grandma's First Baptist Church."

On the other hand, we had many people who came expecting a First Baptist Church experience but got something totally different. We always knew the guests because they were the ones in a suit or dress with silver dollar eyes.

I totally understood the desire to change the name of our church and, personally, I agreed. It made sense. But I had already been through so many battles, I really didn't want to fight this one.

We had relocated the church. We built a building that doesn't even have a steeple, for crying out loud. We transitioned from wearing suits and ties to wearing jeans and flip-flops. We stopped using an organ, piano, and orchestra and plugged in a rock band. We dropped Monday night visitation and challenged our people to invest in their neighbors. We stopped using a hymnal and started projecting our words on a screen. We replaced pews with theater chairs and used a pub table instead of a pulpit.

Rather than having a come-forward invitation, we asked people to come to the back and talk with a pastor if they wanted to take the next step. We moved from Sunday school classes that met on campus to small groups that meet in homes. I stopped preaching topical sermons and started preaching verse-by-verse through a book or passage. We moved from a deacon body and monthly business meetings to a board of directors with an annual business meeting. We moved from about sixty committees to three. We moved from formal to informal. Missions were no longer a department of our church; it was the DNA that ran through every fiber of our church. We changed so much so fast that I really didn't know if I had it in me to try and take another hill as big as a name change.

However, soon we would move from being one church in one location to one church in many locations and we wanted each location (campus) to have the same identity. Since there is a First Baptist Church in every city, USA, we couldn't open a campus called First Baptist Church.

Since Smyrna was in our name, we were restricted to a local identity. So, in order to open other campuses and maintain a consistent identity, we needed a "glocal" name.

A church can open other campuses and use different names. A "small" church in Alpharetta, Georgia, called Northpoint Community Church has opened campuses called Buckhead and Browns Bridge and I guess you could say they're doing OK. So, naming multiple campuses the same name isn't a necessity, but it was the strategy we were pursuing.

Before, I wasn't willing to attack this animal because I didn't feel we had a compelling reason. I didn't want to change the name because it wasn't cool enough or even because of the baggage it carried. It could easily be justified, but it could also be perceived as shallow and a pricey bullet to shoot.

But now things were different. We had a compelling reason to change our name. We didn't need to change our name because we were running *from* something; we needed to change our name because we were running *to* something. We needed to change our name so we could expand by opening other campuses for the glory of God among the nations.

If we go back to Matthew 16, when Peter declared that Jesus was the Christ, the Savior, the Messiah, the Son of

God, Jesus told Peter, "Because of your confession, you're starting a new chapter of life. So, I'm changing your name to Peter."

Jesus does not identify the church according to names like Baptist, Methodist, or Presbyterian; the church is identified by those who confess Jesus as Savior and surrender to Him as Lord. Our identity should be in Jesus, not any other banner.

Scripture has many examples of people's name being changed. Abraham, Sarah, Benjamin, Esther, Daniel, Gideon—these heroes of faith weren't always called by these names. Their names changed with a new chapter in their life.

Even though we now had a compelling reason, I still felt we would receive a lot of push back. So, we drove in the slow lane, trying to bring everyone along at a good pace. We started casting the vision to our board and then extended it to larger and larger circles until we finally had a couple of church-wide meetings.

We had small focus group meetings to allow the people to have input into our new name. Over and over, "life" was the word people kept using to describe what was happening at First Baptist Church. John 10:10 was the Scripture that seemed to resonate with what was happening; "I came that they may have life and have it abundantly."

In the end, we chose to use LifePoint because our purpose is to point people to a Christ-centered life. We don't want to make converts; we want to make disciples who live a Christ-centered life.

Our board unanimously approved our name change. Our plan was to go slow with actually replacing the signs and referring to our church as LifePoint. So, we decided to unveil the new name to the church and tell them we would wait six months before we rebranded as LifePoint.

But, people were so excited about what God was doing, they started pushing us to change the signs and rebrand immediately. To my knowledge, we didn't lose one person because of changing our name. God was obviously bringing His people into alignment with His heart for the nations.

The Reward of Adopting the Nations

Not long after this, we opened our first local campus, Stewart Creek Campus, about four miles from our Smyrna Campus. Then, we sent our first international team to Bangkok to start LifePoint Bangkok. Six months later, we sent Kyle to Brussels to begin paving the way for

LifePoint Brussels. After our second Sacred Gathering, God had moved us from a local church to a "glocal" church in a matter of a couple of years.

Several years prior to our second Sacred Gathering, Amy told me she really thought we needed to adopt a little girl from China. Her heart was broken for orphans and she knew the one-child policy in China had created a major issue with little Chinese girls. So, she asked me to pray about adopting. I told her absolutely not. I was about as interested in adopting as I was in having a kidney stone.

Our boys were almost grown. We didn't need a baby-sitter for the first time in years. We had freedom that we hadn't had in years. The last thing I wanted was to have more kids at this stage of life.

So, I told Amy I wasn't even going to pray about it. I was like a horse headed to the barn. I was done. Amy didn't nag me; she just went over my head and began to talk to the Father about her heart's desire.

When we went to India to establish our partnership in Bihar, I was preaching in a small village on the Nepalese boarder. After I finished preaching, we went to the river for a baptism service and then back to the village pastor's hut for dinner.

As I was moving my food around on my plate (I have no clue what it was), the pastor's two-year-old daughter began to play with Amy. Amy had taken her picture with a digital camera and showed it to her. She was enamored with both the picture and Amy. It was during that moment that God clearly revealed His will for us to adopt a little girl from China.

I didn't tell Amy what I felt in that hut. I wanted to spend some time in prayer to make sure it wasn't the spicy Indian food I had eaten. I didn't want to get Amy's hopes up only to let her down. So, we came home and I began to really pray hard.

After several months of failing to convince God I didn't need to adopt, I finally said, "OK, Lord. There is a little girl in China who doesn't have a mom or dad to tuck her in at night and tell her they love her. I can do this to serve an orphan." But, I felt God clearly reveal to me that His plan for us to adopt wasn't simply about an orphan who needed a home.

So, I thought it must be about Amy. She worked hard to put me through both college and seminary. Now, after all the sacrifices she had made, I wasn't willing to sacrifice for her. Again, God clearly revealed to me that serving Amy was a noble reason, but it still wasn't the reason.

Finally, God revealed to me that His plan was for us to adopt because He wanted to adopt people from every language, tribe, and nation into His kingdom. God wanted my family to become a visible illustration of His heart and His kingdom.

LifePoint needed to see a multicultural family because God's heart is for the church to become multicultural.

Up until that point, LifePoint had a couple of black members and even a couple of Hispanic members, but we were really a white church. Dr. Martin Luther King Jr. once said that 11 o'clock on Sunday morning was the most segregated hour in America. Sadly, it was true then and it's still a reality in most churches today.

Revelation 5:8–14 reveals the purposes of God for all of history.

> And they sang a new song, saying, "Worthy are you to take the scroll and to open its seals, for you were slain, and by your blood you ransomed people for God from every tribe and language and people and nation, and you have made them a kingdom and priests to our God, and they shall reign on the earth." (Rev. 5:9–10)

His future eternal kingdom will be full of people from every tribe, nation, language, and skin color. This is what history is all about. It's what a baby born to a virgin in a cave in Bethlehem is all about. It's about redeeming and filling heaven with a beautiful diversity of people of all colors and languages to worship Him and live in His glory for all of eternity.

Now, I was ready. I could do this. Like everything else in the world, this wasn't about me or Amy or even an orphan girl in China; it was about the glory of God.

So, Amy and I adopted not just one little girl from China, but also a little girl from Ethiopia and a little boy from China. Our family looks like the United Nations. But, more importantly, it looks a little like the vision of heaven we're given in Revelation 5.

We adopted Jadyn, our Chinese daughter, in 2007. Five years later, I've lost count of the number of LifePointers who've adopted domestically and internationally. Our kids' ministry is a kaleidoscope of color and nationalities. But, it's not just because of adoption.

One of the most amazing rewards we are experiencing for our obedience is the fact that LifePoint is becoming a very multicultural church. It was almost like God said, "OK, if you're going to get serious about My heart for the nations, if you're going to obey My command to go to the nations, then I'm going to bring the nations to you."

Today, when I stand on the stage, I don't see a sea of white; I see red and yellow, black and white, and they are all precious in His sight.

As I write this, I have just received news that we are now seeing second-generation believers in Bangkok as the Thai believers our missionaries have led to Jesus are now leading their friends to Jesus. We don't have front-row seats to what God is doing in Bangkok; we're actually in the game. What a reward!

But, it's not just about sending people over there; it's about sending people into every domain of their life. We are blessed to see people embrace their job, their school—wherever God has planted them—as their mission field. The cost of obedience has been high, but they don't even compare to the rewards. And it all started with a costly "ask" called the Great Commission.

✝ *LifePoints* . . .

LifePoint has simply been blessed because of its obedience and passion to be the hands and feet of Jesus, whether in Belgium and Bangkok, or in Smyrna, Tennessee. LifePoint Church has been through much growth and some challenges along the way as any church will, but the resolve and focus of the leadership to reach the community has never wavered. **—Marc**

For two years we couldn't come to any consensus on what needed to be built. Only after we stopped seeking to expand our buildings, God began to send us to other locations with groups of people to start new work. Not a larger campus . . . but more campuses (churches) of people to have influence where there wasn't a healthy reproducing church—that is what God wanted. **—Kyle**

~~~~~~~~~~

I think LifePoint's transition from First Baptist Church, Smyrna, has allowed for people that would have never stepped a foot in the door of a Baptist church to come to LifePoint. The name change did not change LifePoint's identity, but I think was a great way to reach an entirely different group of unchurched individuals. **—Cortney**

Moving Forward . . .

1. What is the most difficult decision you have ever had to make for God?

2. How can you pass on the lessons you learned to help other people grow?

Chapter 8

Go-ology

Brothers, join in imitating me,
and keep your eyes on those who walk
according to the example you have in us.

(Philippians 3:17)

IN THE EYES OF his peers, Brian is a success by every standard. He's the executive vice president of a successful manufacturing operation. He has a wonderful wife and two great kids. He has a nice house and a new pickup truck. In Tennessee, a new pickup truck is a standard of success. But Brian thinks differently than most men. He isn't driven by titles and cash. He's driven by something bigger.

Brian and I began coaching football together several years ago as a way to minister to kids and families. Neither of us had the time to add something else to our plate. But, both of us had coaching backgrounds and saw this as an opportunity to use our skill set and passion to serve God.

Every year, we discuss hanging up our whistles so we can have more time for our families. But, when we talk about the boys we've baptized and the families we've reached, we just can't seem to walk away.

Most youth coaches are trying to live out their glory years through the lives of their sons. But, neither Brian nor I have a son on our team. Our goal is to use our God-given passion for football to make God famous.

Like many other LifePointers, Brian put his "yes" on the table before he was asked the question. So, Brian didn't hesitate when God led him to leave the business world and enter the world of education. His goal isn't to have the initials CEO after his name. His goal is to mentor and shape the lives of young men and women to be warriors for the global glory of God.

Go-ology 101

I'm grateful for the thousands of Christians who sacrifice jobs and money to move to a different culture for the glory of God. LifePoint has many missionaries living in other countries. But, missionaries aren't just people who have to visit their family on Skype; every Christ follower is a missionary.

Rarely a week goes by that I don't have someone come to me and tell me that they feel God is "calling" them to missions. Now, I know what they mean. They mean they feel "called" to go live in a different context and culture to tell people about Jesus. But, I want to challenge you to think about the language we use. When we talk about Kyle or Seth being "called" to missions, this suggests that only those who move are "called" to missions, as if they are the only ones with a calling.

This is important because how we think determines the way we live. If we think some are "called" to missions and others aren't, then we'll be content to pay for others to do missions for us. But, when we realize we're all "called" to missions, everything changes.

If Christ has called you into relationship with Him, you are called to be a missionary. The call to discipleship is a call to missions.

Go-ology is a word I like to use. We go because we are sent by God. God is a sending God. The greatest example is God sending His Son to be a cross-cultural missionary on planet Earth. But there are plenty of other sending examples in the Bible. From Abraham to Moses to Paul to you, God's people are always being sent into the world on a mission.

We organize mission experiences throughout the year for our people to get on a plane and go help our partners or campuses multiply disciples, leaders, and churches, but I really don't like to call them "mission trips" because missions isn't a trip; missions is life.

Our people aren't limited to living out their calling on an airplane with a passport. Being a Sending Church means we send our people on mission into every domain of their life. Like your community, Middle Tennessee is full of people who will never show up at LifePoint or any other church. So, rather than waiting for people to come to us, we must go to them. Rather than focusing on getting people to come to the building, our churches must focus on sending people out of the building.

Going to ball fields, schools, neighborhoods, and the marketplace isn't just some church growth outreach method; it's normative Christianity. Going is simply living like Jesus lived. Claiming Jesus and not living sent in every domain of life is foreign to the Bible. A first-century Christian wouldn't even recognize Christianity that is an addendum to life. It's everything or it's nothing.

That's why Brian and I have coached football for the last several years. I don't have the bandwidth to coach. I want to spend more time with my wife and kids. But, if I'm going to have the moral authority to challenge people to live sent, then I must live sent.

Live What You Believe

You may hear similar words in a Christian song or see similar words on a Christian T-shirt or bumper sticker. This is a great challenge, but it's a needless challenge because, in reality, we all truly live what we believe.

If we believe salvation is all about us, then we'll expect God to serve us, take care of us, and bless us. But, if we believe salvation is all about God, then we will live for His glory. You truly do live what you believe and how you live reveals what you truly believe.

I have no clue where you are on the spectrum of personal missionary engagement (living sent). But, no matter what your skill set, gifting, passion, or education, you have the same responsibility every pastor and missionary has—to hear God's voice, embrace His assignment, and go.

In his letter to the Romans, Paul challenged Christians to watch him and follow his example:

> Be imitators of me, as I am of Christ. (1 Cor. 11:1)

Don't do a drive-by on this verse. Pause and think about it for a moment.

Are you living a "watch me" life?

If everyone in your church lived the way you lived, what would your church look like?

If they loved the people in your community like you, and invested in them like you, what would people think of Jesus and your church?

Do like I do, live like I live, talk like I talk . . . sounds like Paul might have been a little arrogant. But, he wasn't arrogant at all. This is exactly what discipleship is all about. If you can't say "watch me, do what I do, think like I think, say what I say," then something needs to change.

I tire of hearing Christians make excuses for living a mediocre life. I also tire of hearing false humility. "Don't keep your eye on me; keep your eyes on Jesus." Yes! People should definitely keep their eyes on Jesus. But, like Paul, we should take responsibility for living a sent life, not a perfect life, but a sent life for the glory of God that challenges others to follow our lead.

Although Oswald Chambers died in 1917, he has become a friend to many Christians. In his classic devotional, *My Utmost for His Highest*, he said:

The way we continually talk about our own inabilities is an insult to our Creator. To complain over our incompetence is to accuse God falsely of having overlooked us. Get into the habit of examining from God's perspective those things that sound so humble to men. You will be amazed at how unbelievably inappropriate and disrespectful they are to Him.[10]

To refuse the responsibility of living a life worth following is rebellion and unbelief. So, stop acting like the superstar athlete who denies he's a role model because he doesn't want to live responsibly. God has directed us to be role models for our friends, families, and churches, and we can't opt out of this responsibility.

Every Christ follower must move from customer of the church, to owner of the vision, to a missionary sent into their everyday domains and circles of influence. As a result, people move from being managed to being released. When this happens, watch out!

What Keeps Us Going and Going

A few years ago, Energizer had an ingenious marketing campaign revolved around a rabbit called the Energizer Bunny. That little bunny always entertained me during Tennessee Titans and Tennessee Volunteers football games (there have been many Saturdays and Sundays when I needed extra entertainment).

You know what keeps our batteries charged at LifePoint? Transformed lives! Don't misunderstand, we don't challenge our people to live sent so people can have better lives. We challenge our people to live sent because when God transforms lives, God gets glory. It's all about God, not people. The glory and fame of our awesome God charges our batteries.

I've heard many good definitions of worship, but one of the best is simply "revelation and response." When God reveals Himself, we have no option but to respond in praise or repentance. So, we try to keep stories of transformation before our people so they will respond in worship to our God who redeems and transforms.

We believe telling and celebrating these stories is key to helping your church become a Sending Church. When you see these great stories of redemption and transformation unfold, you need to flood every outlet you have with the story—video, Facebook, Twitter, e-mail, blog, and word of mouth. But, make sure the focus is on the God who transforms, not the people who are transformed. That will help keep the "Go" in your "Go-ology." Dave's story is one of my favorites:

I didn't go to church nor did I spend a lot of time with those who did until one of my friends saw a biker ride posted online and asked me if I wanted to ride. I said, "A church?"

When Pastor Pat walked in front of my bike, I didn't know who he was at the time. Neither did I realize that I had obscene stickers on my windshield until we stopped to eat, and I thought, "Oh boy!" On the next ride I covered up the stickers.

After the first ride, I told my friend, "If we ride with the church, maybe we should actually go to the church." So, the following Sunday we did. Of course we did what most non-Christians would do—we sat in the back and didn't speak to anyone. At the time I didn't know what I was doing, but Jesus did.

I started talking to some of the people we met on the ride and got to know them really well; Mark, Don, Vince, and Barry, just to name a few. At the time, Mark was a greeter at LifePoint. I stood with him one day and Mark said, "If you're going to stand up here, I'm going to get you a name tag." I said, "NO!"

One Sunday, when I walked in the door, Mark handed me a name tag and I think that was the start of me getting to know God. I gave my life to Christ the Sunday before Mother's Day 2005, and was baptized a few weeks later.

Not long after Christ invaded my life, I had a heart attack. While at home recovering, I heard a knock at the door. Mark and Barry came to check on me. We talked for a while and Mark said they had something for me—a check for $2,000. This was a collection taken up among the Son Runners—the biker group from LifePoint. Of course I broke down in tears.

Eight years later I'm on the First Impression Team—I help with baptisms, put the baskets out for the offering for first service, and I actually stand in front of the main entrance greeting people and handing out bulletins.

I know without a doubt that I would not be where I am today without these men and women and, of course, without Him. Because of His grace and glory, my name is written in the Book of Life.

Dave's story is incredible. He is a different person (and biker). His appearance hasn't changed . . . well, he does have a little more ink on his body now. But, his heart has been totally transformed by the power and grace of God. The Holy Spirit effectively drew Dave. Jesus redeemed

Dave. And, He did it through a group of people who were committed to leaving the building and living a sent life through their passion for motorcycles.

The Son Runners are only one way that LifePointers follow their passions in order to be missionaries in our community. Coaching football is another. Don't have a narrow view of how God might use you as a missionary. Be yourself. Follow your passions and let God use you to impact the world.

Transformation Starts with a Conversation

LifeWay Research conducted a study in 2012 about the beliefs and behaviors of Christians concerning sharing their faith in Christ with non-Christians. This is what researchers discovered:

- Eighty percent of people who attend church at least once a month believe they have a responsibility to share their faith with non-Christians.

- Seventy-five percent say they feel comfortable sharing their faith.

- But 61 percent of those had not shared their faith in Christ with a non-Christian over the previous 6 months. And 25 percent said they had shared their faith only once or twice.[11]

The dismal results of the survey are even greater when you factor in the halo effect, a research principle that people tend to underreport negative behavior and over-report positive behavior. We do love our halos, don't we?

The majority of Christians today simply aren't passionate about sharing their faith. This is a problem, but it's not the real problem; it's a symptom of the real problem. Historically, we have implemented all kinds of behavior modification plans and programs to try to motivate people to do something their heart is not passionate about doing. And how is that working for us?

> For no good tree bears bad fruit, nor again does a bad tree bear good fruit, for each tree is known by its own fruit. For figs are not gathered from thornbushes, nor are grapes picked from a bramble bush. The good person out of the good treasure of his heart produces good, and the evil person out of his evil treasure produces evil, for out of the abundance of the heart his mouth speaks. (Luke 6:43–45)

The real problem is a heart problem. So, to reverse the numbers, we must target the heart. And even though the

Bible clearly teaches that people without Christ will spend all eternity in a real place called hell, that reality shouldn't be your ultimate motivation for sharing the gospel.

Our ultimate motivation for sharing the gospel must be deeper than people and their needs; it must be about God's glory and obedience to His commands. That's why theology is so important, because theology affects how you think, and how you think determines how you live. Again, we definitely live what we believe.

When we read Paul's letter to the Romans, we see the heart of an evangelist. Maybe you have heard of a cardiac MRI (Magnetic Resonance Imaging). The cardiac MRI is a safe, quick, and noninvasive way to get a great picture of your heart in action. Paul's letter to the Romans gives us a look at his spiritual cardiac MRI.

Paul wanted to go to Spain because they'd never heard the gospel. So, he wrote this letter to ask the Romans to support him on this missionary journey. Did you notice he was not afraid to ask for support? Romans is really a missionary support letter. Paul writes to remind us of God's mission for every Christian—and thus, every church.

Paul could have come out of the gate talking about what he was going to do (mission). But he waited until Romans 15 to do that! He could have also explained how he was going to do it (strategy). But, before he spoke of the mission or the strategy, he talked about the "Why" behind his passion to preach the gospel. And his passion for preaching the gospel is clear throughout the letter. He shared the gospel because of what he believed:

> For I am not ashamed of the gospel, for it is the power of God for salvation to everyone who believes, to the Jew first and also to the Greek. For in it the righteousness of God is revealed from faith for faith, as it is written, "The righteous shall live by faith." (Rom. 1:16–17)

Here is what Paul believed about the gospel and the reasons why he was not ashamed:

1. The Gospel Is Powerful—*Capable of transforming anyone at any time.*
2. The Gospel Is Salvation—*Redemption from the danger and destruction of the soul.*
3. The Gospel Is for Everybody—*Men, women, and children of every tongue, tribe, and nation.*

How could you possibly be ashamed if you really believe these three truths deep in your soul? How about that for simple theology? If you really believed Romans 1:16, your heart would explode for people. And maybe, like Paul and Peter and John (and every disciple who walked with Jesus), you would even be willing to die for the sake of the gospel.

Marginalized Christians

First-century Christians didn't have a great reputation. They were considered uneducated and simple. I mean, who would be so foolish to follow a homeless carpenter who ended up being executed on a cross? Some even believed they were cannibals because they talked about eating the body and drinking the blood of Jesus. Sounds like an episode of *The Walking Dead*.

It's obvious that many Christians today are ashamed of the gospel. In America, we live in an age of religious pluralism and face mounting pressure to keep our mouths shut. Our personal faith in Christ, as well as our desire for our friends, neighbors, and coworkers to know Him, must be our dirty little secret. Or so we're told.

So, we have a decision to make; are we going to remain silent for the sake of tolerance, or are we going to be obedient for the sake of the gospel? If you truly believe the gospel, then your decision is already made. You live what you believe.

My friend Ed Stetzer wrote a cover article for *Christianity Today* about living out your faith in a religiously pluralistic world. He did a brilliant job of getting down to reality:

> As a follower of Christ, I must live and proclaim that message, or I am not really a follower of Christ. To say, "You can be a Christian as long as you do not share the gospel" is nonsensical. It would be as ridiculous as saying, "Go ahead and be a Muslim, just don't submit to Allah." Or, "Be an observant Jew, but do not follow Torah." Or, "You are free to be a Buddhist so long as you make no effort to follow the eight-fold path." As Charles Spurgeon once said, "Every Christian is either a missionary or an impostor."[12]

Paul lived in a world that looked different from ours, no doubt. But the religious pluralism was the same, if not worse. Mythology, Astrology, and the Imperial Cult (worship of politicians) were big in Roman culture. And the corresponding pressure to keep your mouth shut about your Christian faith caused Paul to spend more nights in jail than a Los Angeles public defender.

Even though Paul was imprisoned, chased out of town, laughed at, ridiculed, stoned, and left for dead on the side of the road, he still said, "I am eager to preach the gospel

to you also who are in Rome. For I am not ashamed"
(Rom. 1:15–16a).

Paul's heart was not governed by his concern for personal safety or spending time in prison. He didn't care what people thought or said about him. He was so passionate about the gospel that he said he'd literally go to hell if the Jews would get saved (Rom. 9:3). That kind of passion is hard to grasp. Paul was willing to go to hell to see people saved. I just want people to be willing to go to the cubical next door.

A person willing to go to hell for someone else is pretty hard to intimidate. He wasn't just willing to give up his reputation to share the gospel; he was willing to give his eternity. I have to admit—I couldn't say that.

Theology Fuels Go-ology

The gospel simply means "good news." The good news is so good because the bad news is so bad. The bad news is that our sin separates us from God and damns us to a real place called hell and there's absolutely nothing we can do about it. All the money in the world can't buy a ticket out of hell. We can't do enough good works to outweigh our sinful actions, thoughts, words, and deeds. It gets even worse:

> For the wrath of God is revealed from heaven against all ungodliness and unrighteousness of men, who by their unrighteousness suppress the truth. (Rom. 1:18)

Paul tells us that, because of our sin, we deserve the wrath of God. You won't find that sermon in the "seeker sensitive section." We love to talk about the love of God, and we should because our finite minds can't even begin to grasp the depth of His infinite and unconditional love. But, talking about the love of God is only half the gospel.

If we want to preach the whole gospel, then we must talk about the love of God, but we must also talk about the wrath of God. When people understand how serious God takes sin, His hatred and wrath against sin, then His grace and love takes on a completely different meaning. All of a sudden, salvation isn't just about me; it's about the glory of God that was attacked by my sin. Do you see why the bad news is so bad?

Enter the gospel, the good news. We're doomed and damned because of our sin and there is nothing we can do about it. The good news is, you can stop trying because Jesus already took care of it on the cross. That's what the cross is all about.

I often get asked why Jesus had to suffer so much. It's a good question. I mean, as horrific as the movie *The Passion of Christ* was, it couldn't do justice to the true suffering of Jesus. Jesus had to suffer so much because He was suffering the wrath of God being poured out for the sins of all who surrender to Him. It's called the penal substitutionary atonement. Below is a great explanation:

> If I were to go to your house and break your china, you may tell me that you forgive me, but in doing so you had to absorb the cost of the broken china. Someone has to pay for the broken china, either me or you, if you forgive me. The cost does not just go into oblivion. Likewise, God did not just wave His hand over our sin when He forgave it, He must Himself absorb the full cost of the injustice done.[13]

Jesus paid the penalty for our sin when He died as our substitute. This is sometimes referred to as the vicarious atonement because a "vicar" is someone who stands in the place of another. So, Jesus death was "vicarious" because He died my death.

Do you see why Jesus' death and resurrection is such good news? But it's not good for everyone; it's only good for those who surrender to Him. Paul addressed this clearly in Romans 1:19–32. He said all men are sinners and are under the wrath of God and will be separated from

God for eternity unless they believe and have faith in the sacrifice of Jesus on the cross.

Paul wrote to the Roman church to help them understand the truth of the gospel. He hoped the result would be a new passion for leveraging their influence to share the gospel and send people all over the world. He hoped their theology would fuel their go-ology.

Do you see why theology is so important? What you believe determines how you think and how you think determines how you live. If you understand and embrace the gospel, then you can't help but live a sent life.

Like Paul, we're set apart for the gospel. As I discussed in chapter 4, many churches still, unknowingly and, I believe, unintentionally, practice an Old Testament ecclesiology and an Old Testament view of delivering the gospel. Rather than following the example of Jesus and Paul and going to people, we try to advance the gospel by inviting people to come to us (or our church services).

Many churches even design their worship services for lost people, thinking performances at the building will help people follow Christ. We want to design quality worship services at LifePoint, but they're primarily designed for believers to worship and grow. Our services are relevant to lost people but designed for believers.

Do we really think that lost people will flock to our buildings once a week? Are lost people looking for cool churches where you can wear jeans and listen to U2? Is that the only roadblock to them experiencing the love and power of Jesus? No! Bricks, mortar, big screens with movie clips, and amazing rock bands with lights and smoke machines do not do evangelism. Church models do not do evangelism, whether they are traditional, contemporary, or something in between. Real people influence real people for Jesus Christ and His gospel.

Don't let the programs of the church rob you of what it means to be set apart by God for the glory of God. Let your theology inform your go-ology.

⚡ *LifePoints . . .*

Recently, some friends of ours from the baseball field were separated and on the brink of divorce. She started joining us for church. Her husband started coming with her several weeks later. They got saved and baptized. They are now serving in worship arts and small groups! This is just a microcosm of so many other stories like this throughout the LP body, but that one was a really cool one for us to be able to witness personally. **—Dann**

LifePoint is the church of second chances—we accept people no matter their background or life situations. We talk to them, not about them. God has changed me by pushing me to be Jesus on my street and in my neighborhood, rather than being worried about people attending my church. **—Eddie**

~~~~~~~

Living a missional life has changed my life. LifePoint has helped me to realize that everything I do is for missions and for God's glory. He will be glorified in all we do. Being on mission every day in my season of life (raising three missionaries in my home) is both a challenge and my calling. **—Amy**

Moving Forward . . .

1. What places/people in your community are you the most passionate about?

2. What would it look like to engage those places/people with the gospel on a higher level?

Chapter 9

Warfare

Jesus said to them again, "Peace be with you.
As the Father has sent me, even so I am sending
you." And when he had said this, he breathed on
them and said to them, "Receive the Holy Spirit."

(JOHN 20:21–22)

I'VE ALWAYS HEARD THAT nothing worthwhile is easy. During LifePoint's transition to becoming a Sending Church, I realized these words are not just some trite cliché; they describe reality. But, when I hear stories like Erica's, I'm like a mom holding her newborn baby in her arms; I forget all the pain because the eternal trajectory of countless lives has been changed:

Many people have become Christ followers because LifePoint is committed to being a Sending Church. When LifePoint sent me and eight other college students to be interns at our Bangkok Campus, I met a Thai girl named Diane who was a student at Bangkok University, which is located across the street from our campus. She was attracted to LifePoint because she wanted to practice her English in the classes offered at our campus. We instantly connected and became good friends, even though communication was difficult because her English wasn't great and my Thai was worse.

After a few weeks, Diane began to open up and share personal aspects of her life. Her sister died a few years ago and her mom has had a very difficult time dealing with her loss. She spoke of how it broke her heart to see her mom so sad. One night she said, "I want to have the joy that you all have. I want to be loved like you love each other." It broke my heart to know that she didn't feel joy and love, but it also excited me to know that God was drawing her to Himself.

I knew what we were in Thailand to do, but now it became real. Jesus said, "In the same way, let your light shine before others, so that they may see your good works and give glory to your Father who is in heaven" (Matt. 5:16).

Two weeks after our first conversation, Diane surrendered her life to Jesus. She is now attending LifePoint Bangkok and growing to become more like Jesus every day.

We try to communicate over Skype, but it's so hard because of the language barrier. But, I'm going back to Thailand in March to spend a year and I'm so excited to continue our friendship! This is what God calls each of His followers to do, to let their light shine among all men so that they may see and believe.

Our mission is to be a Sending Church. Sending isn't just a program in our church. It's not just a part of who we are. It's the essence of who we are. It's our ambition, our passion and, we believe, the reason we exist.

I don't believe being a Sending Church is unique to LifePoint; I believe it's God's purpose for every church. Each expression of the local church is commanded to live as sent people for His kingdom.

Every church is different. We're located in different places with different cultures. We have different opportunities and responsibilities. We have different resources (people, partners, materials). So, the "How" will always be unique to each church's DNA. But, the "What?" of the mission is the same—sending.

The biblical foundation for living as a sent people is loud and clear. Jesus gave it to His disciples immediately upon His resurrection. The clarion call for every believer and every church is found in Matthew 28:19–20 and Acts 1:8. I've already referred to it many times in this book. I refer to these passages many times throughout the year in my preaching because it's our marching orders. But Matthew and Acts are not the only places that reveal Jesus' Great Commission.

Mark recorded it this way:

> And he said to them, "Go into all the world and proclaim the gospel to the whole creation." (Mark 16:15)

In John 20:21–22, Jesus said:

> "Peace be with you. As the Father has sent me, even so I am sending you." And when he had said this, he breathed on them and said to them, "Receive the Holy Spirit."

In this passage, there are three interconnected parts moving outward:

1. Peace—The work and mission of Jesus starts in me. I am no longer in a battle with Jesus, trying to hold on to my past or my possessions. Peace has been declared by Him and received from Him. I now enter into a battle **for** Jesus instead of **against** Jesus. I am free from the anxiety and restlessness that comes from living a self-centered life.

2. Sending—I am now sent on a mission into the world just like Jesus was sent. And, I am not alone. The "me" becomes a "we"—I am on a team made up of every Christ follower. We have been sent by Jesus to all nations (people groups) on the planet. This is the reason Jesus saved me. It's my purpose and responsibility.

3. Power—We don't have to be discouraged by our level of ability or power to accomplish this mission. When Christ embraces us, He gives us the supernatural ability to make His mission happen. He gives us the ability to do even greater things than He did through the gift of the Holy Spirit. We have supernatural ability to do the impossible—change the world.

The sent mandate is the commission for every Christ follower on the earth. But the manifestations are a beautiful, diverse representation of the power of God.

God didn't just give Paul the mission; He gave him the motive behind the mission! For all of us who want to be a Sending Church, these words should inspire us for His glory. I love these verses:

> Now to him who is able to do far more abundantly than all that we ask or think, according to the power at work within us, to him be glory in the church and in Christ Jesus throughout all generations, forever and ever. Amen. (Eph. 3:20–21)

I'm a dreamer, but I will never be able to outdream God. He has done things beyond what we could have ever schemed, planned, or plotted. We've had some success at attracting more people and seeing lives changed. But when we started our transition, becoming a Sending Church wasn't even on our radar until our first Sacred Gathering in 2004. And even then, we really had no clue what it meant to be a Sending Church.

Don't Hate the Bride

As I said in chapter 1, I have little patience for people who bad-mouth the church. The church is the bride of Christ. Now, I've officiated a lot of weddings and I've seen a lot of beautiful brides who look perfect on their wedding day. But, we all know the imperfection is simply hidden behind a veil and a lot of makeup. There is no such thing as a perfect bride.

In the same way, we all know there is no such thing as a perfect church. I've attended many conferences and walked away feeling like that church was perfect. I was envious because they seemed to have it all together. Then, as I got to know some of the leaders and pastors of the churches that I envied, I began to realize they had just as many problems and headaches as I do.

There is no such thing as a perfect church because all churches are made up of imperfect people. But, Jesus created the church, empowers the church, and loves the church. It's His bride.

My wife, Amy, is a gift from God. I know a lot of people think I'm perfect. Sometimes, I even convince myself that I'm about as close as I can get. But, when my head starts to swell, Amy is always quick to reel me in from fantasyland.

Amy knows all my flaws and, believe me, there are many. She can tell me my blind spots every day, but if you start talking about my flaws in front of her, you had better get ready to rumble.

I confess the bride of Christ has underachieved in a big way when it comes to the mission of God in the world. We are at the point where books, strategies, or even

Sacred Gatherings will not move us to where we need to be. Our only hope is divine intervention, and that's exactly what happened at LifePoint. Jesus intervened to change our story.

God wants the same results—lives radically changed and people radically sent—for your church. But, again, the "how" is unique to your context. The obstacles and the opposition will be obvious. "We don't have the money. We don't have the leaders. Our people are stuck in tradition." You can fill in that blank with hundreds of excuses. But, that puts you in the best position possible because God will get great glory when it happens.

The "Rudy" Church

As the church, we have put ourselves, sad to say, in the position of underdogs. But when the underdog wins, people look for reasons why—and God becomes famous. He has brought LifePoint light-years forward but as we say in Smyrna, "We ain't there yet."

Our leaders have made connections with other churches that are living as sent people in their own unique way under the Spirit's direction. So God's best story has not been written yet. And I think it could be yours.

A great underdog story gives hope to all of us. Why? Because most of us are average people, with average abilities, living average lives. Everyone loves to cheer for the underdog. We love to see the little guy overcome the odds and beat up the bully. That's why the movie *Rudy*, based on the true story of Daniel "Rudy" Ruettiger, is one of the top sports movies of all time.

Rudy was a classic underdog story about a boy who grew up in a small steel town with a dream of playing football for the Notre Dame Fighting Irish. Why anyone would dream of playing for the Irish, I'll never know.

Rudy wasn't big enough, fast enough, or good enough to play for the Irish, but he refused to give up. And his tenacity and commitment paid off. He spent more time on the bench than a Supreme Court justice, but his dream never died. He finally played the last three plays in the last game of his senior season against Georgia Tech. In his last play he sacked the quarterback and became one of only two players in Notre Dame history to be carried off the field by his teammates.

As famous as Rudy's story is, it's not the most famous underdog story of all time. The most famous underdog story is from the Bible and it's a good description of what we have experienced at LifePoint as we came to a deeper understanding of why God created the church. It's probably the most famous OT Bible story: it's the story of David and Goliath.

Often when a team or athlete faces unbelievable odds, they're referred to as "David versus Goliath"—many times, they don't even know it's a story from the Bible. The story has just become synonymous with an underdog narrative.

God called LifePoint to some amazing things and, like David, we had a choice to make. We could go hard after what God called us to do or we could watch someone else live the dream of being used by God to make a difference.

The Rest of the Story

David was a "Rudy." No one expected much from this young shepherd. His brothers were off fighting in the battle against the Philistines in the Valley of Elah. I've stood in the middle of this valley imagining the story unfold in my mind. I even brought home some rocks from a dry creek bed running through the valley to remember this epic story.

The Israelites were camped on one side of the valley and the Philistines on the other. Meanwhile, back in Bethlehem, David's dad, Jesse, asked him to take some food to his brothers. Looking at David's heroics will, hopefully, inspire you to go hard after the things God has called you to, even when it means fighting a battle that appears too big to win. (Read the entire story in 1 Samuel 17.)

As David arrived, he heard a deep, raspy voice insulting Israel and, more importantly, Israel's God. Just like every kid his age, he got excited because he thought he was about to see a fight. But, he was more than a little surprised to see the entire Israeli army shaking in their sandals. That's when he realized that this was no ordinary enemy.

Goliath was 6 cubits and a span, which translates to 9'9". Can you imagine the payday this dude would command in the NBA?

The Philistines (Goliath's teammates) wore huge coats of body armor that hung from their shoulders to just below their knees. Goliath was covered from head to toe in 225 pounds of body armor. The head of his spear weighed about twenty-five pounds and he also had a shield the size of a normal man. Big vision requires facing down some big giants.

Facing the Giants on God's Mission

Any time you tackle something worthwhile, you'll also face off plenty of giants. Some you can name and prepare for. Others will surprise and disappoint you. But all of us who fully embrace God's sending mission should understand the source of the opposition. Paul identified the enemy of God's mission:

> For we do not wrestle against flesh and blood, but against the rulers, against the authorities, against the cosmic powers over this present darkness, against the spiritual forces of evil in the heavenly places. Therefore take up the whole armor of God, that you may be able to withstand in the evil day, and having done all, to stand firm. (Eph. 6:12–13)

My friends, Ed Stetzer and Jerry Rankin, wrote an incredible book that every Sending Church leader should read. The title even inspires me: *Spiritual Warfare and Missions: The Battle for God's Glory Among the Nations.*

They identify two lines of Satan's defense against the glory of God and the gospel. Satan is blinding people in your neighborhood, as well as the world, from God's greatness and His plan as summarized in John 3:16.

1. The Internal Line—This is what keeps us fighting in our churches, spiritually weak, and inwardly focused. Satan wins most of his battles at home, inside the church. But Ephesians 6 explains that Satan is a supernatural military strategist like the world has never seen. He is not satisfied with one line of defense against God's glory and the gospel. Some churches will make it across the first line. So, he has a second line of defense.

2. The External Line—This line includes keeping nations closed to the gospel, Christian persecution, political opposition to the gospel, and lack of awareness of people groups. Once you break out of the Satan's first line of defense in the local church, the battle continues to rage.[14]

Rankin and Stetzer summarize:

> The devil is opposed to the extension of God's kingdom on the earth and is actively seeking to deprive God of being glorified among the nations through the proclamation of the gospel. . . . No doubt his mission is clear: to keep lost people lost.[15]

I want you to see one of the most common strategies of Satan in my experience of LifePoint becoming a Sending Church. Hopefully this will help you see that you are not crazy (another one of Satan's methods) and help prepare you for the battle of becoming a Sending Church.

Satan's mission is to keep lost people lost and one of his methods is discouraging Sending Church leaders though their critics. David wanted to defeat Goliath for God's glory. You'd think people would cheer David on and throw him a party, but instead, he was criticized. And the first criticism came from his brother. At times, people closest to you and people you least expect become your most devastating critics:

> Now Eliab his eldest brother heard when he spoke to the men. And Eliab's anger was kindled against David, and he said, "Why have you come down? And with whom have you left those few sheep in the wilderness? I know your presumption and the evil of your heart, for you have come down to see the battle." (1 Sam. 17:28)

Your critics will question your motives. This hurts the most. I have been wrong more than once about the methods I chose. I have enthusiastically run forward with the wrong plans—but seldom have I felt it has been for the wrong reasons. To me that is the most personal and painful criticism.

To serve God well as a Sending Church pastor, I have to let my pride and ego die. That is the only way I can stay focused on the mission. And I must be willing to let people I trust ask me tough questions. But, if I make the mission of God all about me and my leadership, I will constantly be hurt by people's criticism. And I will carry anger and resentment toward the people that God has called me to love and lead.

David's older brother wasn't his only critic; his beloved king, Saul, also disrespected David for an entirely different reason. Saul questioned David's experience and ability.

> And David said to Saul, "Let no man's heart fail because of him. Your servant will go and fight with this Philistine." And Saul said to David, "You are not able to go against this Philistine to fight with him, for you are but a youth, and he has been a man of war from his youth." (1 Sam. 17:32–33)

Your critics will question your experience and ability. I learned this the hard way. I thought serving God meant everyone would pull for you. But, I quickly learned when you swim against the current, you have a lot of resistance. Yet, we can learn from our critics, right? There is usually a hint of truth in any criticism if we're brave enough to uncover it.

Saul was 100 percent correct in his criticism, by the way. David was young and inexperienced. Goliath was older and seasoned. On paper, it wasn't a fair fight. I go back to my previous point: If you take criticism personally, then you are the problem, not your critics.

Let me unpack: David was too young and experienced to fight Goliath—that's a fact. Saul was not questioning his character (as was Eliab), but he was questioning his competency.

I don't have the ability or experience to lead a church to the place where God has led LifePoint. LifePoint was the first church I ever pastored. I had no real résumé. I had been a youth pastor for several years. I bet you're just like me and might even be just like the young shepherd boy, David. You probably have a huge selection of reasons to question your credentials.

After Saul tried to tell David all the reasons he couldn't fight this battle, David laid his résumé in front of him. In fact, let me correct that. David laid God's résumé in front of Saul:

> And David said, "The LORD who delivered me from the paw of the lion and from the paw of the bear will deliver me from the hand of this Philistine." And Saul said to David, "Go, and the LORD be with you!" (1 Sam. 17:37)

David was a mere teenage boy and yet he was about to destroy a major threat to Israel's national security. But, David understood a powerful truth: 1 + God = A Majority.

Don't waste your energy hating on your critics. Love them. Learn from them and let God fight the battles. David said, "The Lord who delivered me . . . will deliver me."

This is important because, I guarantee, if you decide to lead your church to become a Sending Church, you better expect and be prepared to face down a lot of criticism. You will be criticized for

- going somewhere else instead of here
- spending money there instead of here
- changing your name (if you should)
- going to one country instead of another
- opening another campus or starting small groups
- starting another church
- giving money or resources away to people who don't deserve it
- raising money
- not talking care of "our own"
- going on too many mission trips
- and much more . . .

David faced his most intimidating critic when he faced Goliath. Goliath was familiar with intimidating most of his enemies into defeat. He talked some real smack with David:

And when the Philistine looked and saw David, he disdained him, for he was but a youth, ruddy and handsome in appearance. And the Philistine said to David, "Am I a dog, that you come to me with sticks?" And the Philistine cursed David by his gods. (1 Sam. 17:42–43)

People will criticize your strategies. Goliath's criticism was similar to Saul's, but the heart was much different. Israel's representative in the battle was unimpressive along with the weapon he brought with him.

Goliath basically said, "Are you sending a boy with a knife to a gun fight with a world champion? If you were sending him to defeat a dog, he might have a chance." The smackdown was on as Goliath basically laughed at David and said, "Is this all you've got?"

Goliath spoke as a "roaring lion" (sound familiar? 1 Pet. 5:8) who intimidates his prey with his loud mouth. How many leaders have been discouraged by Satan's lies and accusations? I know there are times where I have been.

Satan was called the "accuser of our brothers" in Revelation 12:10. The Hebrew word for "Satan" is "slanderer" in the Old Testament. He talks smack. He insults us. He tells us we are stupid, unworthy, and that no one likes us.

David refused to let critics set his agenda. He refused to be intimidated or back down. He was determined to do what God called him to do. That kind of boldness is inspiring and it came from a mere teenager.

David faced Goliath with reckless abandon because he knew the battle was God's, not his. For forty days this giant had challenged the Israelites. Day after day, the soldiers listened to this arrogant loudmouth disrespect Israel and her God. But, they didn't do anything about it because they were intimidated.

But, David wasn't intimidated. He was a warrior. He knew that no matter how big and powerful Goliath was, God was bigger and more powerful. So, David stepped on the battlefield and killed Goliath. Let me rephrase that, David stepped on the battlefield and God won the victory. David was obedient and courageous and God was made famous.

Imagine if David had the same fearful and apathetic attitude of the rest of the Israelite army. He wouldn't have been criticized but we would not have this story—this gift from God to help us learn incredible lessons about God's heart, power, and mission.

When I served as associate pastor in Texas, there was a man who constantly criticized the pastor. He was wealthy, loud, and sort of a big shot in the city, which made him a little intimidating. One day, he came into the office bashing the pastor. The pastor listened patiently and then asked a simple question, "When was the last time you led anyone to Christ?" The man got mad and walked out because he couldn't answer. Often, the same critics who question our character, credentials, and competencies have none themselves.

Front Line or Supply Line Missionaries?

Our battle is for the souls of every man, woman, and child on the planet. If that battle is not a giant, then the church is not paying attention or engaging the mission on a high level. At LifePoint, God has called us to amazing stuff that's beyond our ability and resources. We have faced many giants and will continue to face them as we move forward.

We have challenged our people to engage and embrace the mission of God through tithing, giving generously above the tithe, and going. This is not a business; it's a battle! And people who attend LifePoint are not customers or even just members, they're missionaries.

We don't apologize for asking big things from our people. We don't want to make church members; we want to make disciples who live in obedience to God's Word.

God has clearly given the church the mission of going to all nations, taking the gospel so people can be redeemed. He has commissioned the church to be a Sending Church, to raise and train pastors and missionaries and send them out.

I once heard that you are either on the front line or the supply line; meaning, you are either on the front line in Belgium, Bangkok, China, or some other country, or you are on the supply line providing the necessary funds and resources to make it happen. But, I don't really agree with that. It sounds good, but I don't think it's accurate.

I truly believe that every believer is saved and set aside to be one both the front line and the supply line. The call to Christ is a call to missions. The invitation to discipleship is an invitation to join Him in the mission for His global glory.

So, if you're a believer; you're a missionary. You're called to be on the front line. You might not be directed to move to China or India, but you are called to the front line of your job, school, home, neighborhood, and every other domain of your life. Every believer is a front line Christian or they don't understand what being a Christian is all about.

But, it doesn't stop here. Every believer is also a supply line Christian. We should be fighting on the front line and, at the same time, giving money and providing resources so people who have been directed by God to move to China or India or some other country can fight the battle in that region of the world. So, if you've surrendered your life to Jesus, then you better be on both the front line and the supply line or you're being disobedient.

John wrote a letter to one of his spiritual children named Gaius:

> Beloved, it is a faithful thing you do in all your efforts for these brothers, strangers as they are, who testified to your love before the church. You will do well to send them on their journey in a manner worthy of God. For they have gone out for the sake of the name, accepting nothing from the Gentiles. Therefore we ought to support people like these, that we may be fellow workers for the truth. (3 John 5–8)

John was Jesus' best friend while He was on this planet. So, he knew Jesus' heart well. He was the only original disciple left. All others had been murdered.

John was the most influential pastor in the world and he was identifying young men, training them to be pastors, and sending them out as missionaries. They'd leave their jobs to move and start churches all over the world.

This was a vital part of the first-century church. They'd go start churches and follow the same pattern of training pastors and sending them out as missionaries.

John praised Gaius for supporting the missionaries he sent from his church because his support allowed them to preach the gospel. I doubt that anyone has ever named this "Rudy" as their favorite Bible character—no one has called him a hero. But he is to me because of how God used him. Notice, John told Gaius that, because of his support, people were being sent—he was partnering in spreading the gospel. How important is that?

John learned this model from Jesus. His ministry was totally supported by friends like Mary, Martha, and Lazarus. This is the vision and model God has called LifePoint to follow. We didn't invent it; we're simply following the model of the early church.

God has called us to identify, raise, and train missionaries, to go make disciples. We will continue planting churches all over the world in places like Belgium, Bangkok, China, Seattle, etc. Our goal is for these churches to follow the model and become Sending Churches by raising, training, and sending out missionaries.

My Bible says that God established the church to be an unstoppable offensive force for the global glory of God in this world, not a weak, intimidated, and irrelevant religious club. My Bible records the words of Jesus saying, "As the Father has sent Me; I am sending you." A Christian not living sent is foreign to the Bible. It's not a possibility.

✝ *LifePoints . . .*

We changed our missions strategy because people far from Christ need to be filled with His life. We changed our name, not because our previous name was boring or old, but because it was the best way to streamline the movement of our church and its gospel mission among the nations. **—David**

~~~~~~

If God can empower and enliven the pastors and congregation in a "rag-tag, motley crew, hybrid mixture of citified and countrified group of people" in Middle Tennessee . . . then it can happen anywhere. **—David**

~~~~~~

There will be spiritual warfare and a necessity of prayer when God is doing work through people. Satan doesn't want to see lives changed. Anytime we can make a difference it should be an encouragement as to what God can do with a willing church and willing leadership. **—Seth**

Moving Forward . . .

1. What is the biggest obstacle to your church becoming a Sending Church?

2. What are your next steps in addressing the obstacle?

Chapter 10

The Sending Movement

While they were worshiping the Lord and fasting, the Holy Spirit said, "Set apart for me Barnabas and Saul for the work to which I have called them." Then after fasting and praying they laid their hands on them and sent them off.

(Acts 13:2–3)

THE VISION OF LIFEPOINT is to send the church to be the church. I don't know why, I shouldn't be, but I was amazed at how many LifePointers resonated with and rallied around this vision. Imagine if thousands of churches across the US embraced the Sending Church vision and ran hard after the heart of God. Every tongue, tribe, and nation would hear, see, and experience the gospel in our lifetime.

We surveyed a select number of our leaders as part of the Sending Church Project. All of them responded individually to an online survey and were able to speak from their hearts. No one was looking over their shoulders, and they couldn't copy off anyone else's answers. The questions were open-ended so they couldn't hide behind checking boxes. They had as much time as they needed so they could really think about their answers.

Let me tell you—although we still have many issues to work through—after seeing the hearts and thoughts of our leaders, I could not have been more encouraged. God has changed the culture of LifePoint Church. You know how I could tell? Because He has changed the conversation.

I want to invite you to be a part of something big—no, let me rephrase that . . . something God-sized. I am not suggesting the activity of God can be reduced to a formula. Formulas are for recipes and chemistry sets. But, I would love for you to embrace six heartshifts that are critical to becoming the Sending Church God created you to be.

1. Imagine a Jesus Movement

An incredible tsunami of lostness hovers over our planet. People are drowning in their sin, hopeless without the gospel. That's why Christians must go; that's why churches must send. That's why we must start a Jesus movement that flows through local churches worldwide to take the gospel across the street and across the world.

No longer do we have the luxury of half-hearted efforts to add a few new believers here and there. We can no longer think addition; we must think multiplication. Time is short. People are dying all around us. And, if one soul is of incredible value to God, then how valuable are hundreds of thousands of souls? We long to see the rapid multiplication of new believers that results in great movements of God sweeping the globe like an incredible rescue operation through unreached, unengaged, and neglected people groups around the world.

When our hearts become ablaze with the glory of God, our mission efforts will explode into culturally diverse movements (see Acts 2 for an example). And these movements will consist of many disciples being made, many leaders being trained, and many churches being planted.

After seeing what God can do with a few Sending Churches, the thought of a great movement of Sending

Churches blows my mind. But, the last thing I want to do is create organizations or networks to zap our energy (while producing little results). But, if we can combine our knowledge, expertise, and experiences, I'm just crazy enough to believe that we can see a Jesus movement sweep the planet that can literally take the gospel to every tribe and nation in our lifetime.

Northwood Church in the Dallas/Fort Worth area has been a Sending Church for years. Founding pastor, Bob Roberts Jr., defined what he called a "Jesus movement" that fuels my vision to see God do something great. A Jesus movement was first seen in the New Testament:

> Individuals found Jesus, he revolutionized their lives, and as a result Jesus spread from their lives to the lives of their family and friends. Then, so many wound up following Jesus that churches were necessary to assimilate all the people. It was a Jesus movement.[16]

LifePoint Church is displaying the greatness of God to the nations by initiating and nurturing at least seven Jesus movements among seven distinct peoples/places. These peoples/places are representative of the following world affinity groups: Buddhists, Non-Religious Europeans, Non-Religious Chinese, Hindus, Muslims, Tribal Poor, and Non-Religious in the USA.

So what if we all worked together? Sending Churches encouraging each other, praying for each other, learning from each other, believing . . . filled with hope for a worldwide Jesus movement!

2. Start Thinking Upstream

A heartshift always precedes a change in behavior. In the spring of 2008, my great friends, Larry McCrary and Caleb Crider, launched The Upstream Collective (theupstreamcollective.org).

Larry and Caleb were both serving as missionaries in Western Europe when God began to transform their thoughts and gave them a new way of thinking about missions. They embraced the current reality that all was not well in the world of sending missionaries. It became obvious that a couple of things were broken.

First, they believed that many churches had outsourced the Great Commission. Missions had become a program versus the core function of local churches. For all the positive effects of central mission sending agencies, there was one huge negative: the church was forgetting the mission.

As I've said throughout this book, the spiritual implications of outsourcing the Great Commission are huge.

Can you imagine paying someone to obey God for you? As crazy as that sounds, I don't believe it's overstated.

I can understand a church paying someone to service their heating and air conditioning units. And, I am perfectly good with churches having their carpet cleaned by ServiceMaster's or subbing out their accounting work. But the sacred mission of God? The Great Commission? Not on your life!

Outsourcing the mission of God is a fancy way of describing biblical "disobedience." Yet, the business model makes all kinds of sense. Outsourcing is hot! According to one website, the United States outsourced over two million jobs in 2011 for perfectly good reasons.[17] But good, practical reasons to outsource do not make it right, particularly for missions.

Central giving funds for missions make sense. I am by no means suggesting they should be eliminated. At LifePoint we give to various central missions funds of the Southern Baptist Convention because we believe they are an eternal investment. But God has moved us beyond a mind-set of outsourcing missions. At that point, everything radically changed. We give to support missionaries of the International Missions Board and the North American Missions Board, but we also fully own the responsibility of sending missionaries to the nations. We cannot outsource our command to go.

Second, Larry and Caleb believed that churches were not involved with those whom they had sent. Once the church sent missionaries to the mission field via a mission-sending agency, they seemed to be forgotten by their church. The church was forgetting the missionaries.

"Out of sight, out of mind," seems like a trite descriptor of the current reality in the sending world. But with the exception of Christmas or Easter, churches can unplug from the missionaries who need their support.

The challenge of staying connected to the mission and the deployed missionaries is real. Watching video clips and reading brochures makes the mission of God to the nations seem distant. And giving percentages of weekly offerings feels like outsourcing, particularly if that is the extent of our involvement.

The lack of authentic ownership of God's deployed missionaries is staggering. The negative results extend far beyond declining support, prayer, and caring for those sent directly to the nations. It appears that people are no longer being challenged to hear God's direction and embrace His assignment to the nations.

The other implication is that missions is reserved for seminary-trained professionals. No wonder people are backing away. Beyond an occasional missionary speaker to their local church, there is no real face on deployed missionaries or their mission. This leads to apathy and disengagement.

Churches have a responsibility to be a part of sending people and staying involved in their lives. Spiritual accountability, nourishment, and strategic involvement are vital from local churches to deployed missionaries. The health of God's mission depends on it.

3. Think and Act Like a Missionary

The Upstream Collective became a new type of mission organization that facilitates the mission efforts of the local church. This replaces the old-school thinking that a local church supports the mission efforts of the mission organization with a more biblical thinking that the church *is* the sending agency.

Old-School Thinking—

Local Church>Mission Organization>Missionary> Mission

Upstream Thinking—

Mission Organization>Local Church>Mission> Missionary

Notice, in the old school, the local church was far removed from the mission and the missionary—as well as the real activity of God. With Upstream thinking, the mission organization backs up the local church that embraces the mission of God and fully embraces the missionary.

In most Upstream environments, the missionary is coming from the local church. So the connections are real and become a platform for every man, woman, and child in a local church to seriously consider God's directive to be sent to the nations.

A new type of missionary was part of Upstream's conversations. The new missionary does not necessarily need to raise support. Real jobs give them a reason to be in their country and a means to stay in their country. And those real jobs give them access to people with the gospel that professional missionaries do not often have.

I love the mission of Upstream Collective:

Upstream is a collective of missional leaders and their respective churches that identify themselves by a common goal: **to see churches think and act like missionaries.** We believe we can change the world by challenging the traditional mindsets about mission and offering a better, more biblical alternative.[18]

I met Larry and Caleb when they were doing a road trip around the US to talk to churches about these topics. These were the early days of development for what the Sending Church could look like on a broader scale. Our hearts were so in sync that LifePoint and Upstream became strategic partners on a journey to help churches learn from each other what it means to be a Sending Church.

4. Join What God Is Already Doing

I really believe that we are in the early phases of an authentic movement in the US where the people of God own God's mission in new ways.

Larry McCrary describes the trends in Sending Churches:

> Churches are sending people in a variety of ways. Through the marketplace, church-based teams, students, short-term missionaries, traditional mission-sending organizations, etc., the mission of God has multiple delivery points.

LifePoint is one of many emerging Sending Churches worldwide. I learn about more Sending Churches on a weekly basis. Plenty of churches are out there getting it done and helping us understand more and better ways to send missionaries.

Henderson Hills Baptist Church in Edmond, Oklahoma, is one of those Sending Churches (www .hhbc.com/missions). The biggest change at HHBC over the past five years has been a refocus toward unreached people. They have narrowed their focus to reach the 2 percent or less evangelized.

Almost all of their time, resources, and people are going toward the unreached. Mike Wall, the Missions Pastor at HHBC, described the way God is shaking the congregation through a worldwide focus on unreached people:

> God is using the Muslims from North Africa to wreck our lives. We have realized, in sharing Christ with them, that we are asking them to leave their culture, family, and way of life to follow Jesus. In return we are asking ourselves the same question. Are we willing to let go of anything and everything to follow passionately after Christ?

HHBC has found that equipping the number of people being sent from their church is one of their greatest challenges. These people usually have no ministry experience or seminary training. Therefore, they have been forced to create intensive training programs so that missionaries will be adequately equipped to effectively share the gospel.

"Without question, God has strengthened my faith and creativity," Mike said. "My faith in hearing and trusting God to send them to the right places, and creativity to get them there through unconventional means, has grown." No doubt, their vision is God-sized:

> Under the mandate of the Great Commission, our vision is to spiritually equip, financially support, and mobilize the people of Henderson Hills both long- and short-term, so as led by the Spirit to strategically impact the lostness of the world.[19]

The challenge of sending is also a faith challenge. The risk is great and the picture is seldom clear. "The most exciting thing for us has been the way in which God has opened one door at a time, never being in a hurry, but never being late," Mike said. "As churches send, there will be more unknowns than knowns. We have to remember that God knows everything, therefore, we don't have to."

Urbancrest Baptist Church in Lebanon, Ohio, is another Sending Church (urbancrest.org/missions). Recently someone who attended Urbancrest Church said, "You cannot attend Urbancrest without learning about the world and the love Jesus has for everyone in it." The culture of missions is exploding to all age groups as the calling to missions is extended to everyone.

Urbancrest has deployed a total of five international missionary units to Uganda, Germany, and Haiti. Members are planting churches in Hillsboro, Ohio; Kapolei, Hawaii; Cincinnati, Ohio; and Lebanon.

Aaron and Dana Bogan is one example of Urbancrest members living out the Great Commission. The Bogans moved to Jinja, Uganda, with their four children. Aaron, after serving in the Navy, had completed his master's degree in mathematics and was employed as a professor of statistics at Miami University in Oxford, Ohio. Dana is trained as a Registered Nurse. They were living the American dream!

Then, in 2005 Aaron and Dana experienced a life-changing event when they heard the gospel of Jesus Christ. The Holy Spirit effectively called them and they made Jesus their Lord. They began a journey of obedience to the heart of God that radically altered their decision-making process. Shortly after God's dramatic rescue of their lives, He directed them to go to Uganda.

At their commissioning in 2011, Aaron stood with his family on the stage and commented that they were just ordinary people that had been saved by the blood of Jesus and the grace of God. Then he said, "Take a look at us. This is normal for followers of Jesus. We are to follow Him wherever He sends us."

This is the new old normal. It's new because, somewhere along the line, missions became something only for the seminary-trained. It's old because it's normative Christianity that dates back to the beginning of Christianity. It's what Jesus established the church to do and it's what He redeemed His followers to do.

The funding mechanisms that we have traditionally used are wonderful and have given the churches a great infrastructure of missionaries all over the world. Unfortunately, there are not enough missionaries or funding to fulfill the Great Commission with this method. The gospel is to be preached to all peoples, according to the words of Jesus (Matt. 24:14). Revelation 7:9–10 tells us that there will be people from every tribe, tongue, and nation worshipping at the throne of God.

"When God leads everyday people out of a church to other parts of the world, everyone's perspective of the world and God's mission changes," said Minister of Missions, Doss Estep. "This is a biblical mandate and the Spirit of God will direct and transform churches through it. This is the fuel of the church!"[20]

5. Discover Your Church DNA

The DNA of every church—rich or poor, suburban or urban, large or small—is sending. Imagine what would happen if every church embraced their DNA and became the Sending Church that God created them to be! LifePoint, Henderson Hills, and Urbancrest are only a few of the churches embracing this sending movement. I hope you get in on the action.

I humbly embrace the specifics of what God has invited us to do at LifePoint. I don't think that every church in America should send missionaries to Brussels and Bangkok or India. Neither do I think that every church should become multicampus. And, I don't believe that every church should make the exact same transitions mentioned in this book, like changing your name or your pastor preaching in jeans. As a matter of fact, if you can avoid those changes and still be a Sending Church, by all means, avoid! Let me say that again, avoid!

But, I do believe your church should be a Sending Church. That's not my opinion. If it was, you could take it or leave it. But, it's not my opinion; it's God's direction. You can't walk away from this responsibility if you want to walk in obedience to the commands of God.

As you become all God wants you to be, you will face incredibly difficult decisions. And you will likely need to make radical changes in your approach to church. As Jesus explained to the crowd in Luke 14:25–33, there are no easy ways to truly follow Him.

Acts 13 is a significant transitional passage in the history of the Jesus movement.

> Now there were in the church at Antioch prophets and teachers, Barnabas, Simeon who was called Niger, Lucius of Cyrene, Manaen a member of the court of Herod the tetrarch, and Saul. While they were worshiping the Lord and fasting, the Holy Spirit said, "Set apart for me Barnabas and Saul for the work to which I have called them." Then after fasting and praying they laid their hands on them and sent them off. So, being sent out by the Holy Spirit, they went down to Seleucia, and from there they sailed to Cyprus. When they arrived at Salamis, they proclaimed

the word of God in the synagogues of the Jews.
And they had John to assist them. (Acts 13:1–5)

Although the gospel was already branching out
beyond Judaism as Christians scattered all over the world
to avoid persecution, international "sending" started in
the Antioch church. This passage gives us a picture of the
first true Sending Church who prayerfully, intentionally,
and strategically sent people to another culture to multiply gospel influence to the nations.

Act 13 contains several elements that have been a
vital part of LifePoint's transition to become a Sending
Church. I wish I could say we read this passage and followed the pattern God used in the Antioch church, but
we didn't. It really wasn't until later that we realized that
God used some of these same elements to create a sending
environment in LifePoint. What are some of these common elements?

Element #1: Worshipping, Praying, and Fasting: The
discipline of seeking God's heart seems to be a no-brainer,
but it's not. It really didn't occur to us until 2004 that we
needed seasons of intentionally seeking God. I am not
saying we didn't pray, teach prayer, or believe in prayer.
But at times our belief was not reflected in our behavior.

John Piper gives perspective on how prayer fuels the
missionary impulse of the Sending Church:

The chief end of God is to glorify God. He will do this in the sovereign triumph of his missionary purpose that the nations worship him. . . . And he will make that engagement plain to all participants *through prayer*, because prayer shows the power is from the Lord. The range of his powerful engagement in the warfare of missions becomes evident from the range of things which the church prays for in her missionary enterprise.[21]

Fasting was also a critical avenue for us to focus on nothing else but God. Imagine if churches set aside every pursuit and ambition for a given period of time and focused solely on seeking God's heart. We determined to no longer put words in God's mouth—because God actually put His words in our hearts as we fasted to say, "God, more than we hunger for food, we hunger for You."

Element #2: Gifted, Visionary Leaders: These were the best five men Antioch had to offer. The team had a mixture of prophetic and teaching gifts. People in the church had to be overwhelmed that the best and brightest would go elsewhere.

At LifePoint we have experienced that struggle. But God never calls everyone from the base camp—because the operations to develop and deploy disciple/leaders must never stop. God, in the moment, sent two and left three in Antioch.

- Barnabas (sent)
- Simeon
- Lucius of Cyrene
- Manaen a member of the court of Herod the tetrarch
- Saul (sent)

The Antioch church had obviously done a great job discipling and raising leaders. That's our job—to bring them in, raise them up, and send them out. That's why we're here. We're not just about making converts; we're about making disciples and leaders.

Jesus loved the harvest so much that He did not spend all His time harvesting! From the beginning of His public ministry He spent as much time with harvesters as He did with the harvest. Reading His sending plan, as explained in Matthew, gets my blood pumping:

> When he saw the crowds, he had compassion for them, because they were harassed and helpless, like sheep without a shepherd. Then he said to his disciples, "The harvest is plentiful, but the laborers are few; therefore pray earnestly to the Lord of

the harvest to send out laborers into his harvest."
(Matt. 9:36–38)

Jesus described the harvest as "plentiful." The harvest
was also of great value. The harvest, in the minds of Jesus'
original audience, was a gold mine. Nothing was more
vital to life and the local economy as the harvest. So, the
harvest was urgent.

Because of the size and value of the harvest, the job
was too big for only thirteen men, no matter how hard
they worked. Jesus gave those who loved the harvest two
priorities. The first priority was prayer, because in human
terms, success was not only unlikely; it was impossible.

The multiplication of harvesters was the second priority. Jesus gave His earthly life to multiplying harvesters—thus the local church was about praying, raising, and
sending. The Antioch church was just doing what Jesus
willed them to do.

The proof of spiritual growth isn't how many Bible
verses someone knows, but in what they do. The proof of
spiritual vitality of a church isn't how many people they
have, but in how many people they send.

Element #3: Diversity: The naming of these five men
also reveals the racial, cultural, and socioeconomic diversity in the church. Included in the small group was at least
one who was black (Simeon) . . . rich friends of Herod

(Manaen) . . . Jewish (Simeon and Saul), Lucius (from a Greek colony in Northern Africa). Cultural and socio-economic diversity gave the church strength in Antioch.

This is what the church should look like. LifePoint is becoming more and more diverse. As I talked about in chapter 7, my family is a diverse family. I have no doubt that God was at work adding diversity in my own home in order to add diversity to LifePoint.

Unity in diversity demonstrates the power of the gospel. Segregation weakens the church and makes it feel more like a club or clique. Clubs are a part of every community, but they are seldom diverse. Diversity pleases God because it's His heart and diversity glorifies Him. He loves every tongue, tribe, and nation.

Element #4: Teams: John Maxwell warns leaders, "As much as we admire solo achievement, the truth is that no lone individual has done anything of value. The belief that one person can do something great is a myth."[22]

Maxwell has a vision and a voice to multiple leaders who work in teams to accomplish something greater than any individual can accomplish by himself. But, he was not the first person who promoted the importance of teamwork.

Jesus Christ is the ultimate leadership coach, particularly for those who were His followers. He sent His first group of missionaries out in pairs:

After this the Lord appointed seventy-two others and sent them on ahead of him, two by two, into every town and place where he himself was about to go. (Luke 10:1)

Element #5: The Church Is the Sending Agency: Notice, it was the church that received a direction from God to set these missionaries apart and send them out. The church decided who went and where they would go, which is not the norm in today's world.

Today, when an individual or a family feels led to the mission field; they find a mission-sending agency that will send them where they want to go. But, in Scripture, God established the church to be the mission-sending agency.

Again, I love mission-sending agencies and I'm thankful for the impact they've made. So, this isn't to diminish or criticize mission-sending agencies in any way; it's simply to lift high the role of the church.

6. Collaborate

Sending Churches can learn a lot from each other. I hope that God can use this book as a call for churches to resource each other for the sending mission of God. At LifePoint we have benefited incredibly from other churches that have a similar vision and heart. We need a way to collaborate together so we can share resources, ideas, and best practices.

I have listed four different resources that are available now through LifePoint's partnership with The Upstream Collective. But the best resources and opportunities are yet to be created or discovered. Maybe you will be the one that God leads to make this list of resources even larger.

1. The Sending Church Website (thesendingchurch. com). We have a website where church leaders and those interested in sending can read and interact with blogs written about Sending Church topics. The site offers resources that can help the church explore what a Sending Church looks like.

The website is an overarching center for all things Sending Church, from storytelling to theology to resources to community building. It is an introductory point to Sending Church ideas as well as a community resource development tool. The site is useful at all levels of sending, from those just starting to those who have become proficient. Go to the site now. I would love to hear your Sending Church story.

2. Local Roundtables. We host several one-day roundtables in different parts of the country where we talk about Sending Church principles and practices.

These are sponsored by host churches who are committed to sending.

These regional roundtables are meant to introduce churches to the biblical and practical concepts of the Sending Church and to building sending communities among churches. Hopefully you will find people in your own region through these roundtable opportunities. You can find out when and where the next roundtable is on our sendingchurch.com website.

3. The Sending Church Conference. We host the Sending Church Conference once a year. It is a place where the church can bring its staff, mission leaders, etc. to learn some basic elements of the Sending Church.

4. LABS. The Sending Church LAB is a 3- to 4-day training experience designed specifically for teams and individuals heading overseas for short- or long-term missions endeavors. We use the city as a living laboratory to teach basic missiological principles and missionary skills that are to be adapted and contextualized wherever the teams are headed.

The Sending Church LAB focuses on a contextualized urban immersion experience. Teams are thrust into a city in order to learn the skills and tools necessary for navigation. Whether New York or Dubai or Moscow or

Belfast or Tokyo, the principles learned are applicable wherever teams are headed globally.

Next Steps

Before you hurry off to your next meeting, or reach for the next book, I want you to reconsider what God might have said to you through *The Sending Church*. Remember the question I asked Eddie Mosley in chapter 2? I think we all need to be challenged by it again:

> Do you want to play church the rest of your life or do you want a chance to change the world?

If you are ready to join the movement, begin by getting alone with God and reviewing the heartshifts in this chapter:

- Imagine a Jesus Movement
- Start Thinking Upstream
- Think and Act Like a Missionary
- Join What God Is Doing
- Discover Your DNA
- Collaborate

Which one of the six heartshifts are you experiencing the most now? Which one are you experiencing the least? Where does God want you to dig in and take the next steps?

✞ LifePoints . . .

No matter the size of your church, you have a mandate to make disciples of all nations. If that means sending just one from your congregation, do it and don't delay. Giving is good, sending is best. The church will become more healthy and outward-focused as you send. **—Brent**

Many families have given up their comfortable life-styles in order to take the gospel to places where the gospel is not heard. We are raising leaders to take the Good News to our community and across the globe. We are sending the church, to be the church, where there is no church. **—Brenda**

Out of this three-day time of prayer, fasting, and worship, God spoke to our church concerning missions and the seeds of what would become the Sending Church were planted. LifePoint would be a very different church today if this had not happened. **—David**

Moving Forward . . .

1. What resources or opportunities in chapter 10 will help your Sending Church vision?

2. What church can you talk to about sending "best practices" in the next two weeks?

Notes

1. See http://dictionary.reference.com/browse/ unstoppable?s=t&ld=1120 (accessed 11/30/12).

2. David T. Olson, *The American Church in Crisis* (Grand Rapids, MI: Zondervan, 2008), 176, 180.

3. Alvin L. Reid, *Radically Unchurched: Who They Are and How to Reach Them* (Grand Rapids, MI: Kregel Publication, 2002), 23.

4. Bill Hybels, *Courageous Leadership* (Grand Rapids, MI: Zondervan, 2002), 26.

5. Henry Blackaby and Claude King, *Experiencing God: Knowing and Doing the Will of God* (Nashville: LifeWay Press, 1990), 14.

6. Henry Blackaby, Richard Blackaby, and Claude King, *Fresh Encounter: God's Pattern for Spiritual Awakening* (Nashville: B&H Publishing Group, 2009), xi.

7. See http://www.christianity.com/christian-life/ prayer/when-youre-in-trouble-pray-11545844.html (accessed 11/21/2012).

8. See http://www.census.gov/main/www/popclock.html (accessed 11/12/2012).

9. See http://www.nytimes.com/2006/10/06/ us/06evangelical.html?pagewanted=all&_r=0 (accessed 12/7/2012).

10. Oswald Chambers, *My Utmost for His Highest: An Updated Edition in Today's Language* (Grand Rapids, MI: Discovery House Publishers, 1992), November 30.

11. See http://www.lifeway.com/Article/research-survey-sharing-christ-2012 (accessed 11/17/2012).

12. See http://www.christianitytoday.com/ct/2011/april/proselytizingmultifaith.html?order=&start=6 (accessed 11/17/2012).

13. Monegism.com/penalsubstitutionaryatonement (accessed 12/7/2012).

14. For further study of Satan's line of defense, see Ed Stetzer and Jerry Rankin's *Spiritual Warfare and Missions: The Battle for God's Glory Among the Nations* (Nashville: B&H Publishing Group, 2010), 26.

15. Ibid., 51.

16. Bob Roberts Jr., *The Multiplying Church: The New Math for Starting New Churches* (Grand Rapids, MI: Zondervan, 2008), 29.

17. See http://www.statisticbrain.com/outsourcing-statistics-by-country (accessed 12/10/2012).

18. See http://theupstreamcollective.org/what-is-upstream (accessed 12/10/2012).

19. See http://www.hhbc.com/missions (accessed 12/12/2012).

20. See http://urbancrestmissions.blogspot.com/2011/09/new-normal-part-1.html (accessed 12/11/2012).

21. John Piper, *Let the Nations Be Glad, The Supremacy of God in Missions*, Third Edition (Grand Rapids, MI: Baker Academic, 2010), 79–80.

22. John Maxwell, *The 17 Indisputable Laws of Teamwork* (Nashville: Thomas Nelson Publishers, 2001), 2.